Mapping
CENSUS 2000
The Geography of U.S. Diversity

Cynthia A. Brewer
Trudy A. Suchan

ESRI Press
REDLANDS, CALIFORNIA

ESRI
  Mapping Census 2000: The Geography of U.S. Diversity
  ISBN 1-58948-014-7

This atlas was originally published by the U.S. Census Bureau as part of the Census 2000 Special Reports series.
  Brewer, Cynthia A., and Trudy A. Suchan
  U.S. Census Bureau, Census Special Reports, Series CENSR/01-1
  Mapping Census 2000: The Geography of U.S. Diversity
  U.S. Government Printing Office, Washington, D.C.
  Issued June 2001

First ESRI Press edition printed November 2001.

Printed in the United States of America.

Published by ESRI, 380 New York Street, Redlands, California 92373-8100.

Books from ESRI Press are available to resellers worldwide through Independent Publishers Group (IPG). For information on volume discounts, or to place an order, call IPG at 1-800-888-4741 in the United States, or at 312-337-0747 outside the United States.

Contents

Section 4

Hispanic or Latino Origin

White, Not Hispanic or Latino Origin

One Race: White, Not Hispanic or Latino Origin

One or More Races Including White, Not Hispanic or Latino Origin

Acknowledgments

The authors wish to thank managers at the Census Bureau's Demographic Directorate who actively worked on this atlas: Nancy M. Gordon, John F. Long, James D. Fitzsimmons, and Signe I. Wetrogan. At the Bureau's Geography Division, Timothy F. Trainor, Constance Beard, and Deanna L. Fowler prepared geographic base linework and discussed details of map design with the authors. In the Population Division, Claudette E. Bennett, Nicholas A. Jones, Herbert W. Thompson, and Kevin E. Deardorff contributed to the discussion and development of map topics. E. Marie Pees and Janet L. Wysocki prepared special data tabulations. Maps were reviewed by Frank T. Gulino, Theresa B. Andrews, Robert M. Leddy Jr., and Nancy G. Schechtman.

At the Population Distribution Branch, the authors particularly thank Pétra Noble, who prepared, managed, and documented the database that permitted mapping in geographic information systems (GIS) software. Thanks also to Michael R. Ratcliffe for data checking, and to Rodger V. Johnson for editorial assistance. Thanks as well to Donna L. Defibaugh, Todd K. Gardner, Colleen D. Joyce, Paul J. Mackun, and Marc J. Perry.

At the Library of Congress, Kathryn L. Engstrom and Edward Redmond of the Geography and Map Division aided in the study of approximately 40 atlases during preparation of this book.

Nelsa Brown, Arlene C. Butler, and Janet S. Sweeney of the Administrative and Customer Services Division guided graphic design, editorial review, and digital file preparation of the original Census Bureau publication.

The authors also thank David W. DiBiase at The Pennsylvania State University for his many ideas that assisted in planning the atlas. Shaun P. Faith of the Department of Geography's Gould Center at Penn State assisted with the shaded relief for the location map. Thanks also to the many professional cartographers and GIS developers who answered our technical questions and gave comments on early design drafts.

At ESRI, Charlie Frye, manager of the ArcMap™ Products team, provided timely leadership and assistance in making the atlas a reality.

For the ESRI Press edition of the atlas, Christian Harder, Judy Boyd, and Nick Frunzi provided additional support, while Heather Kennedy and R. W. Greene contributed additional editing.

In April of 2000, the U.S. Census Bureau once again conducted (for the twenty-first time in history) the single larg est collection of spatially referenced data ever undertaken in this country. While many people might not immediately think of the resulting population and housing information (organized as it is in massive tables) as spatial or geographic in nature, we in the GIS world recognize that in fact every last bit of this data is linked directly to an exact location somewhere in the United States. This is what makes it such a rich data set from a GIS perspective.

Mapping Census 2000: The Geography of U.S. Diversity, the atlas you are holding, was originally released in limited quantities during June 2001 by the U.S. Census Bureau. It represents a major achievement in digital cartographic production, and we were honored that the Census Bureau chose ESRI® ArcGIS™ software as the primary tool used to prepare the maps. This republication of the bureau's effort is being undertaken by ESRI Press in an effort to alert the GIS user community that the first reports of the Census 2000 data are now available (with even richer sets to follow). But we are also showcasing the superb cartography that has been created by the Census Bureau's GIS specialists.

In the introduction, you'll find useful details about how the maps were created. We hope that this work will inspire GIS users around the world to create maps using their own data that are as well designed, informative, and beautiful as the maps in this atlas. I would also encourage you to visit factfinder.census.gov—the primary delivery channel for Census 2000 housing and population data.

But first, take some time to begin studying these maps. If you're a map lover like I am, I think you'll find that they paint a fascinating portrait of U.S. population patterns and changes.

With warm regards,

Jack Dangermond
President, ESRI

EVERY TEN YEARS a new portrait of America gets painted. The Census Bureau of the U.S. Department of Commerce creates this portrait using numbers, rather than brushes and paint—numbers derived from the millions of census questionnaires filled out by U.S. residents and census enumerators. With the help of software such as geographic information systems (GIS), cartographers then transform these numbers into canvases—maps—that show in intricate detail who Americans are, where they are, and how they work and live.

Saturated with information and color, these maps can, in their own way, be as rich and life-affirming as any Impressionist landscape.

Among the most dramatic of these canvases to emerge so far from Census 2000 are those that show how the racial and ethnic composition of the American population has changed since 1990. A nation founded by immigrants more than two centuries ago has become a hugely diverse nation, whose racial, ethnic, and cultural roots extend to every corner of the globe.

The maps in *Mapping Census 2000: The Geography of U.S. Diversity* show just how varied a nation we have become, and they do so with a level of detail rarely revealed before now.

One reason for this is the nature of the numbers on which these maps are based. This set of numbers goes by several different names, but it is most frequently called "complete count" or "100-percent" data, because it is information that every resident of the country had to supply on April 1, 2000—at least, as close to 100 percent as was possible. It is also often referred to as PL 94-171 data, after the applicable federal statute.

Perhaps the most important subset of this data set is known as redistricting data. Beginning in March 2001, these redistricting numbers were sent to every state legislature in the United States, so that local lawmakers could use it for the decennial redrawing—or redistricting—of federal, state, and local legislative boundaries.

Redistricting is a complex business. Legislative districts must be drawn fairly, so that they represent residents of all races and ethnicities. The Voting Rights Act, and its subsequent judicial interpretations, have increased the need for legislators to have as much information as possible about the racial and ethnic composition of the population if they are to draw new legislative districts fairly. Government services to U.S. residents are also dependent on detailed data about racial and ethnic composition of the population that will receive those services.

Beginning with Census 2000, the U.S. Office of Management and Budget requires federal agencies to use at least five race categories: White; Black or African American; American Indian and Alaska Native (AIAN); Asian; and Native Hawaiian and Other Pacific Islander (NHOPI). For the Census 2000 questionnaire, the government added a sixth category, Some Other Race.

In addition, those who filled out Census 2000 forms could identify themselves as belonging to any combination of any of these six categories.

An added complication—but one that increases the richness of the data—is the fact that Hispanic or Latino heritage or origin is not considered a racial category; it is counted separately from the other six categories. Those of Hispanic or Latino origin could indicate that fact on their Census 2000 form (as they could in 1990), and then further identify themselves by one of the other six categories, or by any combination of them.

There are some limits that redistricting data places on the kinds of maps that can be shown. Nonetheless, with six categories to choose or combine, and with the separate categorization of Hispanic or non-Hispanic origin, the degree of detail about American racial and ethnic heritage that can be derived from Census 2000 numbers is still exceptional.

ORGANIZATION OF THE ATLAS

Section 1 of the atlas shows several perspectives of the total U.S. population in 2000, regardless of race or ethnicity.

Section 2 maps racial prevalence and diversity—that is, which races and ethnicities tend to predominate in various parts of the nation, and which parts of the country are more heterogeneous than others.

Section 3, the largest in the atlas, presents different cartographic views of each of the basic race categories. A series of "One Race" maps begins each category—maps that show the distribution of people who belong to only one race. These are followed by variations on this theme, including the distribution of people of that race in combination with other races. At the end of this section are maps showing the distribution of people who indicated they belong to Two or More Races.

Section 4 maps the population based on the presence or absence of those who identify themselves as being of Hispanic or Latino origin. Because Hispanic or Latino origin is considered an ethnicity, not a race, Hispanic and Latino groups may be of any race.

In sections 1, 3, and 4 of the atlas, four population themes are repeated: Percent Change; Percent of Population; Percent Under Age 18; and Number of People.

Each page of the atlas features county-level detail maps for the 50 states, the District of Columbia, and Puerto Rico. Each page also includes a small state-level map for a simplified view of the population theme.

ABOUT THE MAPS

All the maps in Mapping Census 2000 were created with ArcMap, the desktop cartographic GIS software technology from ESRI. ArcMap is a core building block of ArcGIS, the latest GIS technology suite from ESRI.

Each map was drawn using a customized version of the Albers equal area conic map projection. A caption adjacent to the map legend provides a detailed explanation of the main map title.

Most of these maps are choropleth, meaning that numerical data values are divided into classes and the classes are used to shade areas on the map. (One exception is the Distribution map on page 9, which uses proportional symbols instead of area shading to better illustrate population distribution in the United States.) The map legends on the right side of each page list the range of data values that each color represents.

Choropleth maps are best for showing derived values such as percent or density, and are less appropriate for representing total numbers of people. They are, however, used for totals in this atlas so that counties across maps can be easily compared.

Cartographers employ many strategies for deciding where to place class breaks—that is, where to end one data range, or color, and where to begin the next. Some of the basic approaches include customizing these breaks using characteristics of the data values shown on the map; using arbitrary round numbers; and using breaks that arise from knowledge about the map topic. An additional criterion for this decision is whether

comparison among different maps is more important than emphasizing the class distinctions in a particular map. In this atlas, the maps are designed to both aid map comparison and to provide critical summary breaks within maps. Comparison among maps is emphasized by use of the same categories among maps in a series. The class breaks on the maps were chosen using a combination of arbitrary rounded breaks shared between maps, and national rates for each map topic.

MAP COLOR

A particular color generally has the same meaning within a series so that maps are easily compared. Three different hues in the title bar along the top of map pages are used to group maps into sets across atlas sections: maps that involve the total U.S. population (orange bar), maps that focus on people who indicated only one race on their census form (yellow), and maps that include people who indicated more than one race (pink).

To further aid comparison, the same categories and color schemes are used throughout a map series. In addition, colors were selected to accommodate readers who are colorblind: hues that look different for most colorblind readers are used and shading is arranged from light, for low data values, to dark, for higher or more extreme values.

Overall, the maps use eight different color schemes. Dark purples, blues, and greens are used for the high values on maps. On the Difference, Under Age 18, and Percent Change maps, two color sequences are used to reflect numbers that diverge in opposite directions from a summary midrange value. Both ends of the data range are emphasized with dark colors of two different hues. Light colors are used on these maps around the midrange values to emphasize difference from a U.S. summary rate or zero change. To be consistent with other color schemes, dark purple, blue, and green hues are maintained for the high values on maps with diverging color schemes. Low or negative values are shown in pinks, oranges, and browns.

Data ranges for colors change when breaks are adjusted to include U.S. overall rates specific to the group mapped. For example, a light pink is used to signal ranges between zero change and the overall U.S. change for the group mapped, a range that is different for each change map.

ABOUT THE DATA

As noted, redistricting data restricts the kind of map themes that can be shown: total population; race and ethnicity; and population under age 18, which is derived from the voting-age population counts in the redistricting data. This atlas does not map the more detailed demographic and economic household information that the Census Bureau also collects.

All data sets were rounded to one decimal. Large numbers in the maximum category on the Number of People map legends are rounded up, to the next highest number with four significant digits.

When only one state (or the District of Columbia or Puerto Rico) is represented by a color on a state-level map, the data value and the state abbreviation are reported in the legend rather than a data range (for example, "25.1 (DC)").

The percent of U.S. population for a particular group is calculated using populations for the United States as a whole; for example, the total population under age 18 is divided by the total U.S. population. Note that these summary numbers are not averages of state or county percents. The calculations of the U.S. summary numbers are based on data from all states and the District of Columbia, but do not include Puerto Rico.

There are a variety of ways ethnicity may be incorporated with race groups in the calculation of diversity measures. In this atlas, the calculations for the Diversity maps use categories generally consistent with the Prevalence maps, with the goal of producing a coherent report section. The diversity index mapped is known as Simpson's Index in biology literature.

On the Prevalence maps, people who indicated Hispanic or Latino and also indicated Black, AIAN, Asian, or NHOPI are counted in both the Hispanic or Latino group and in their respective race group. One-half of one percent of the total U.S. population (approximately 1.3 million people) is represented twice on these maps. Therefore, the eight map categories on the Prevalence maps add up to 100.5 percent of the U.S. population.

Unlike the percentage comparisons on the Prevalence maps, the Diversity index calculation is compromised when percentages do not add precisely to 100. Therefore, people who are both Hispanic and Black, AIAN, Asian, or NHOPI are included only in their respective race group on the Diversity maps.

In some cases, an overlay was used to mask counties containing very small populations of the group mapped. This was done because small populations often produce extreme percentage changes that distract from the more reliable pattern seen over areas with greater numbers of people. So, for example, the percent change in populations of Hispanic or Latino origin is not shown in counties where there are fewer than 100 Hispanics.

CHANGES FROM 1990 TO 2000

The 1990 to 2000 Percent Change maps compare data from the 1990 Census—in which residents and census enumerators could mark only one race—to the Census 2000 One Race and One or More Races groups. The data sets from 1990 and 2000 are not directly comparable, but do offer some understanding of population change in individual race groups. There is no 1990 census group suitable for comparison with the 2000 Two or More Races group; that information was not collected in the 1990 census.

Another change for Census 2000 was the separation of the 1990 Asian and Pacific Islander category into two groups: Asian, and Native Hawaiian and Other Pacific Islander (NHOPI). On the relevant Percent Change maps in this atlas, 1990 data was reaggregated to create separate Asian and NHOPI groups for comparison with Census 2000 race categories.

In 1990 and 2000, the Census Bureau used the two nonracial ethnicity categories, Hispanic or Latino and Not Hispanic or Latino. (The terms "Hispanic or Latino origin," "Hispanic or Latino," and "Hispanic" are all used interchangeably.) Both race and ethnicity are mapped in the Prevalence and Diversity section using the following categories: Hispanic or Latino; White, Not Hispanic or Latino; Black or African American ("Black or African American" and "Black" are used interchangeably); AIAN; Asian; NHOPI; Some Other Race, Not Hispanic or Latino; and Two or More Races, Not Hispanic or Latino.

Questions on race and Hispanic origin were not included on the 1990 census form used in Puerto Rico. Therefore, some 1990 to 2000 Percent Change maps in this report show "no data" for Puerto Rico. In 2000, questions on race and Hispanic origin were asked of all people in the 50 states, the District of Columbia, and Puerto Rico, so all maps of 2000 data include Puerto Rico.

Previously published 1990 census data was also reaggregated to Census 2000 geography. This affected only five counties or equivalent entities in the country: Denali and Yakutat boroughs in Alaska; Halifax County in Virginia; and Gallatin and Park counties in Montana.

Location Maps

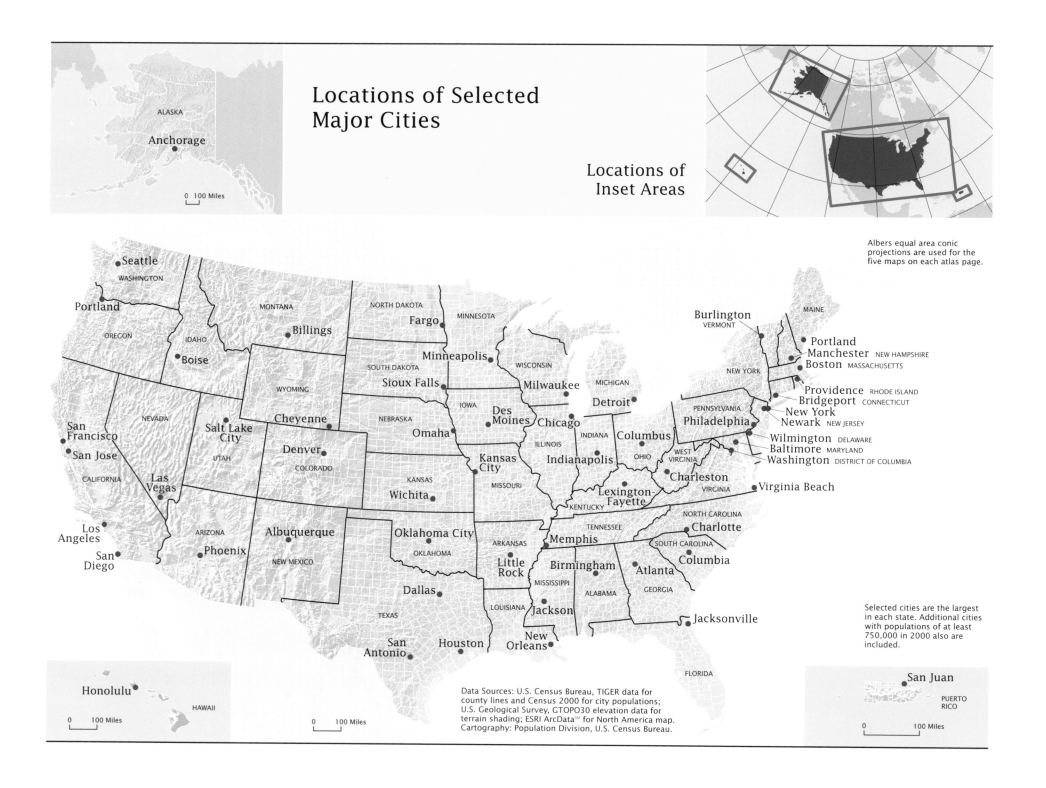

Locations of Selected Major Cities

ALASKA

Anchorage

0 100 Miles

Locations of Inset Areas

Albers equal area conic projections are used for the five maps on each atlas page.

Seattle
WASHINGTON

Portland
OREGON

MONTANA

IDAHO

Boise

Billings

NORTH DAKOTA

MINNESOTA

Fargo

Burlington
VERMONT

MAINE

Portland
Manchester NEW HAMPSHIRE
Boston MASSACHUSETTS

Minneapolis

WISCONSIN

NEW YORK

Providence RHODE ISLAND
Bridgeport CONNECTICUT

SOUTH DAKOTA

Sioux Falls

Milwaukee

MICHIGAN

Detroit

PENNSYLVANIA

New York
Newark NEW JERSEY

WYOMING

Cheyenne

NEBRASKA

IOWA

Des Moines

Chicago

INDIANA

Columbus

OHIO

Philadelphia

Wilmington DELAWARE
Baltimore MARYLAND
Washington DISTRICT OF COLUMBIA

San Francisco

San Jose

NEVADA

Salt Lake City
UTAH

Denver
COLORADO

Omaha

Kansas City

ILLINOIS

Indianapolis

WEST VIRGINIA

Charleston

CALIFORNIA

Las Vegas

KANSAS

MISSOURI

KENTUCKY

Lexington-Fayette

VIRGINIA

Virginia Beach

Wichita

Los Angeles

ARIZONA

Albuquerque

Oklahoma City

NORTH CAROLINA

TENNESSEE

Charlotte

San Diego

Phoenix

NEW MEXICO

OKLAHOMA

ARKANSAS

Memphis

SOUTH CAROLINA

Columbia

Little Rock

Birmingham

Atlanta

Dallas

MISSISSIPPI

ALABAMA

GEORGIA

TEXAS

LOUISIANA

Jackson

Jacksonville

San Antonio

Houston

New Orleans

FLORIDA

Selected cities are the largest in each state. Additional cities with populations of at least 750,000 in 2000 also are included.

Honolulu

HAWAII

0 100 Miles

0 100 Miles

Data Sources: U.S. Census Bureau, TIGER data for county lines and Census 2000 for city populations; U.S. Geological Survey, GTOPO30 elevation data for terrain shading; ESRI ArcData℠ for North America map. Cartography: Population Division, U.S. Census Bureau.

San Juan

PUERTO RICO

0 100 Miles

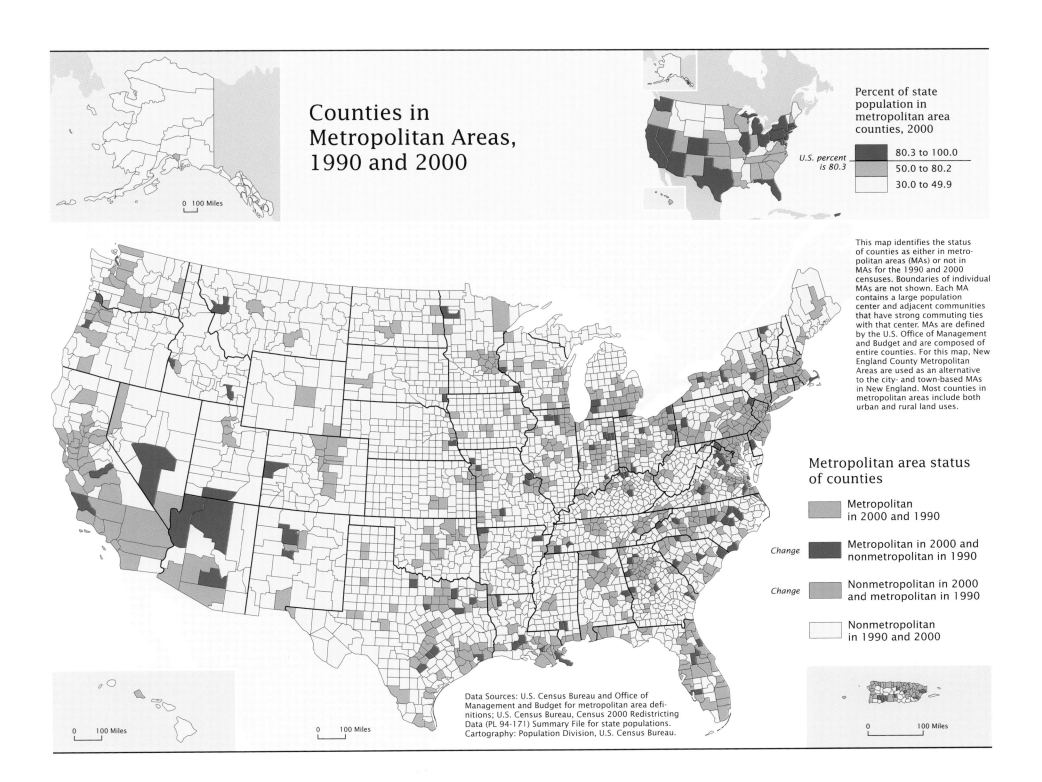

Counties in Metropolitan Areas, 1990 and 2000

0 100 Miles

Percent of state population in metropolitan area counties, 2000

U.S. percent is 80.3

- 80.3 to 100.0
- 50.0 to 80.2
- 30.0 to 49.9

This map identifies the status of counties as either in metropolitan areas (MAs) or not in MAs for the 1990 and 2000 censuses. Boundaries of individual MAs are not shown. Each MA contains a large population center and adjacent communities that have strong commuting ties with that center. MAs are defined by the U.S. Office of Management and Budget and are composed of entire counties. For this map, New England County Metropolitan Areas are used as an alternative to the city- and town-based MAs in New England. Most counties in metropolitan areas include both urban and rural land uses.

Metropolitan area status of counties

- Metropolitan in 2000 and 1990
- *Change* — Metropolitan in 2000 and nonmetropolitan in 1990
- *Change* — Nonmetropolitan in 2000 and metropolitan in 1990
- Nonmetropolitan in 1990 and 2000

0 100 Miles

0 100 Miles

Data Sources: U.S. Census Bureau and Office of Management and Budget for metropolitan area definitions; U.S. Census Bureau, Census 2000 Redistricting Data (PL 94-171) Summary File for state populations. Cartography: Population Division, U.S. Census Bureau.

0 100 Miles

Total Population

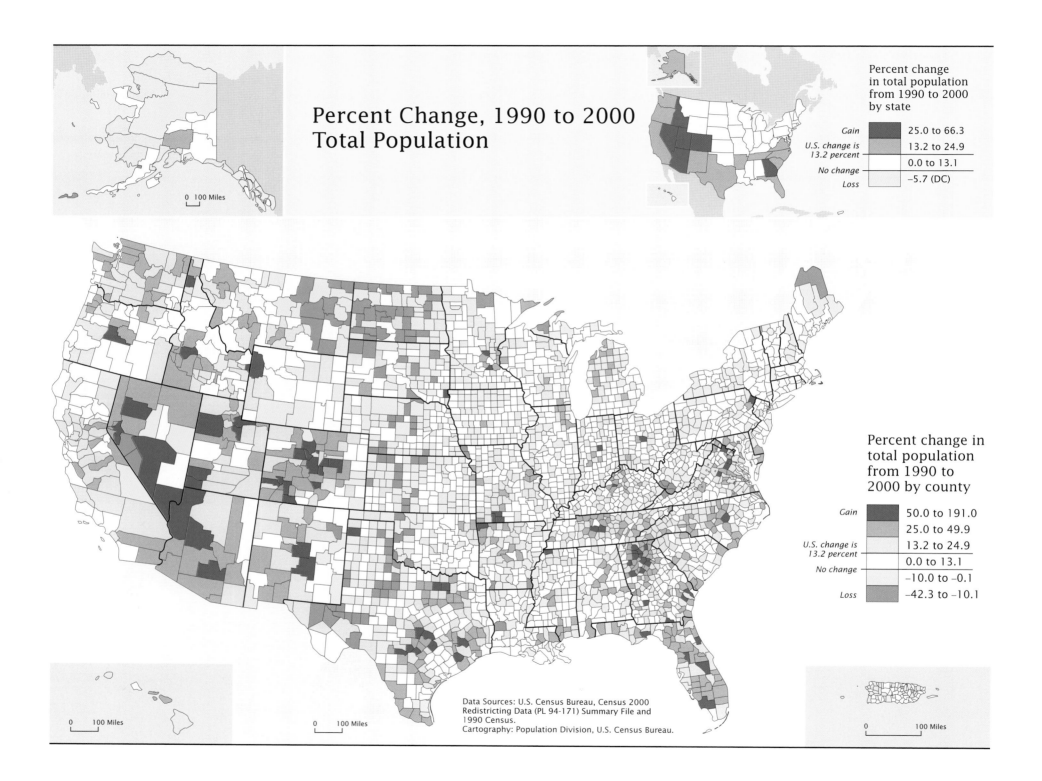

Percent Change, 1990 to 2000
Total Population

Percent change
in total population
from 1990 to 2000
by state

Gain
U.S. change is
13.2 percent
No change
Loss

25.0 to 66.3
13.2 to 24.9
0.0 to 13.1
−5.7 (DC)

Percent change in
total population
from 1990 to
2000 by county

Gain

U.S. change is
13.2 percent
No change

Loss

50.0 to 191.0
25.0 to 49.9
13.2 to 24.9
0.0 to 13.1
−10.0 to −0.1
−42.3 to −10.1

0 100 Miles

Data Sources: U.S. Census Bureau, Census 2000
Redistricting Data (PL 94-171) Summary File and
1990 Census.
Cartography: Population Division, U.S. Census Bureau.

0 100 Miles

0 100 Miles

0 100 Miles

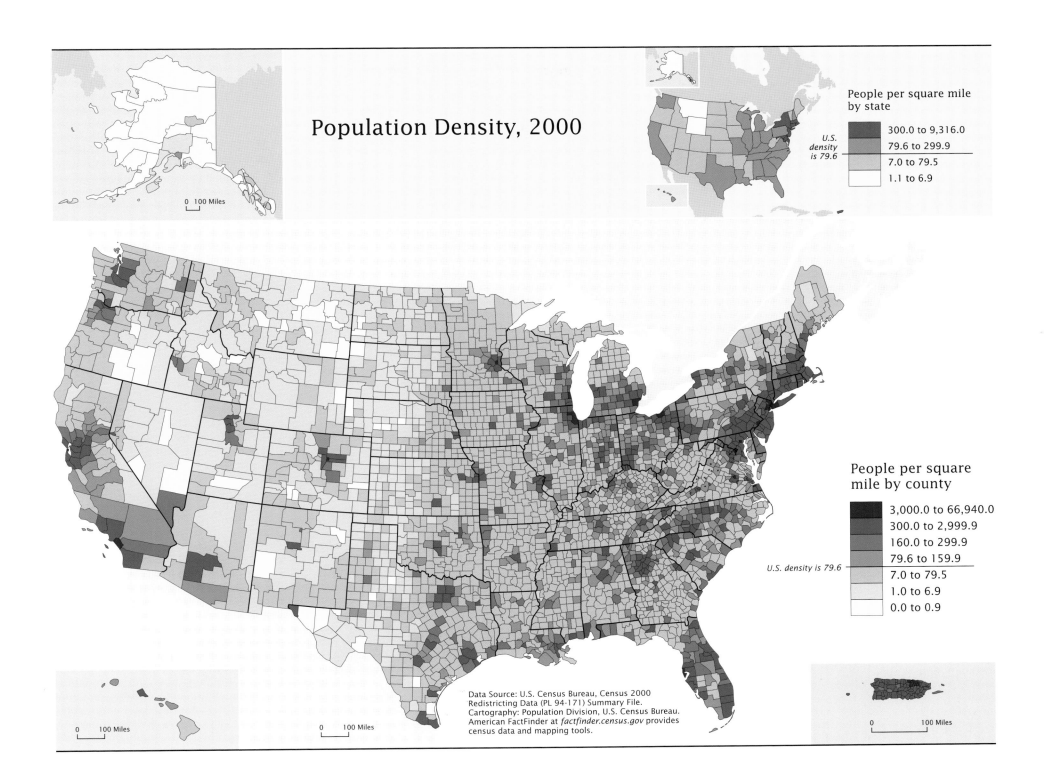

Population Density, 2000

People per square mile by state

U.S. density is 79.6

- 300.0 to 9,316.0
- 79.6 to 299.9
- 7.0 to 79.5
- 1.1 to 6.9

People per square mile by county

- 3,000.0 to 66,940.0
- 300.0 to 2,999.9
- 160.0 to 299.9
- 79.6 to 159.9
- 7.0 to 79.5
- 1.0 to 6.9
- 0.0 to 0.9

U.S. density is 79.6

0　100 Miles

Data Source: U.S. Census Bureau, Census 2000
Redistricting Data (PL 94-171) Summary File.
Cartography: Population Division, U.S. Census Bureau.
American FactFinder at *factfinder.census.gov* provides
census data and mapping tools.

0　100 Miles

0　100 Miles

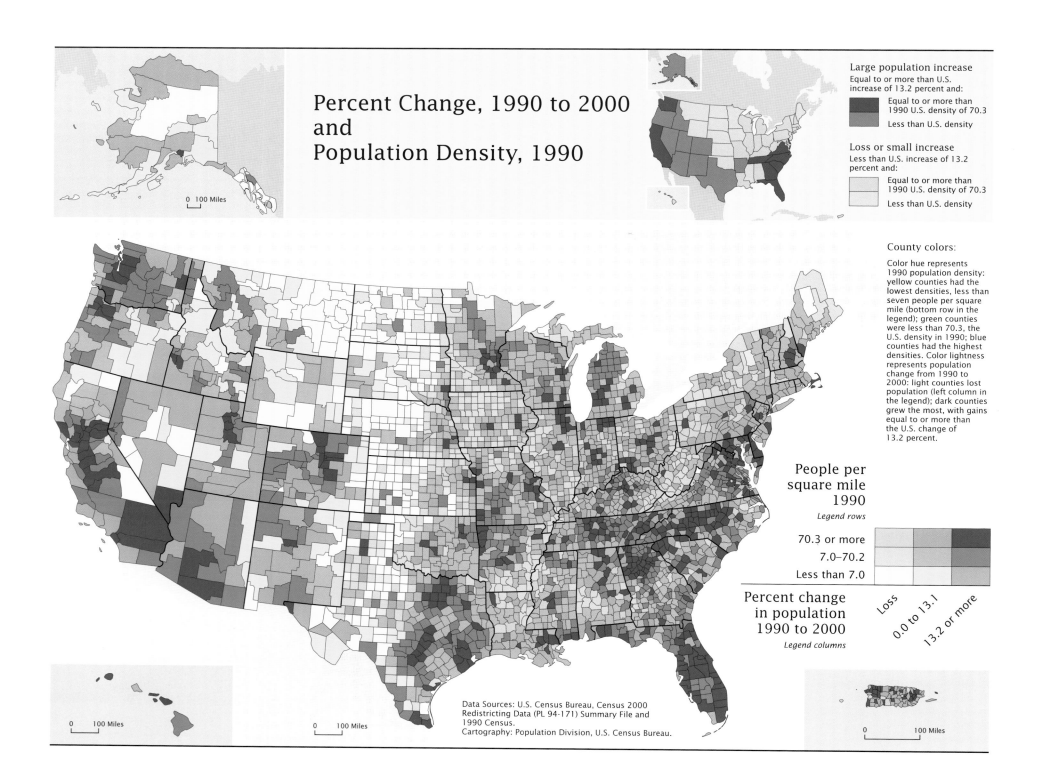

Percent Change, 1990 to 2000
and
Population Density, 1990

Large population increase
Equal to or more than U.S.
increase of 13.2 percent and:

Equal to or more than
1990 U.S. density of 70.3

Less than U.S. density

Loss or small increase
Less than U.S. increase of 13.2
percent and:

Equal to or more than
1990 U.S. density of 70.3

Less than U.S. density

County colors:

Color hue represents
1990 population density:
yellow counties had the
lowest densities, less than
seven people per square
mile (bottom row in the
legend); green counties
were less than 70.3, the
U.S. density in 1990; blue
counties had the highest
densities. Color lightness
represents population
change from 1990 to
2000: light counties lost
population (left column in
the legend); dark counties
grew the most, with gains
equal to or more than
the U.S. change of
13.2 percent.

People per
square mile
1990
Legend rows

70.3 or more		
7.0–70.2		
Less than 7.0		

Percent change
in population
1990 to 2000
Legend columns

Loss   0.0 to 13.1   13.2 or more

0   100 Miles

Data Sources: U.S. Census Bureau, Census 2000
Redistricting Data (PL 94-171) Summary File and
1990 Census.
Cartography: Population Division, U.S. Census Bureau.

0   100 Miles

0   100 Miles

0   100 Miles

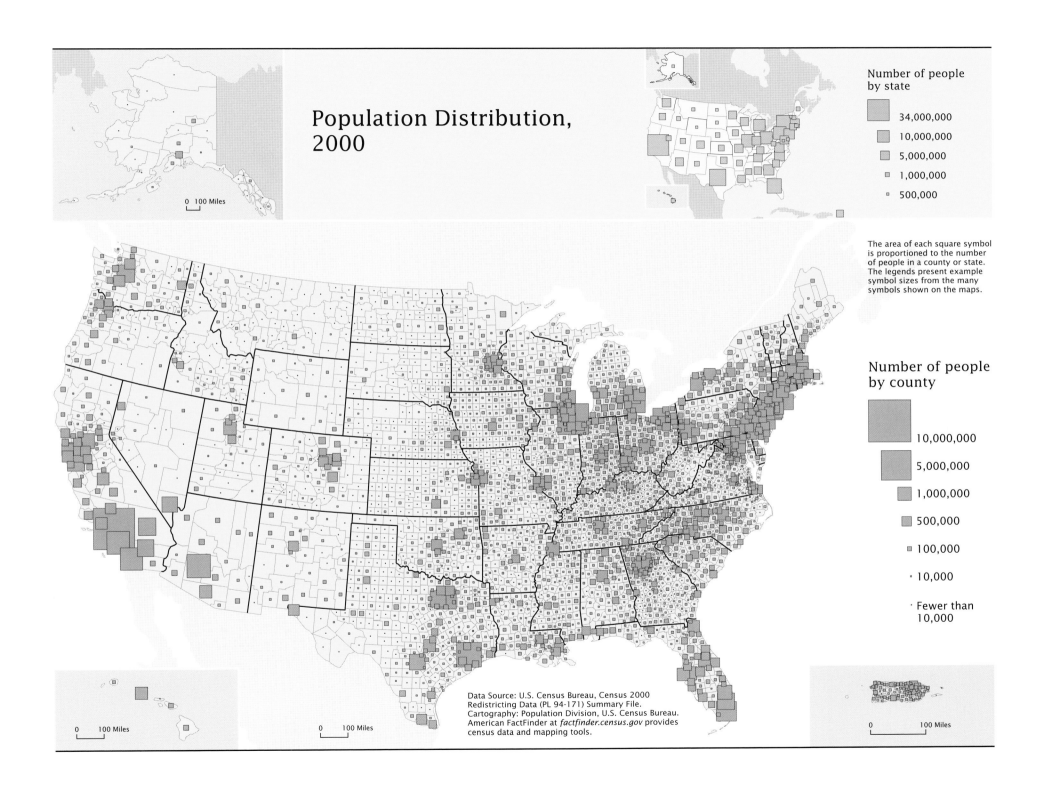

Population Distribution, 2000

Number of people by state

34,000,000

10,000,000

5,000,000

1,000,000

500,000

The area of each square symbol is proportioned to the number of people in a county or state. The legends present example symbol sizes from the many symbols shown on the maps.

Number of people by county

10,000,000

5,000,000

1,000,000

500,000

100,000

10,000

Fewer than 10,000

0 100 Miles

0 100 Miles

Data Source: U.S. Census Bureau, Census 2000 Redistricting Data (PL 94-171) Summary File. Cartography: Population Division, U.S. Census Bureau. American FactFinder at *factfinder.census.gov* provides census data and mapping tools.

0 100 Miles

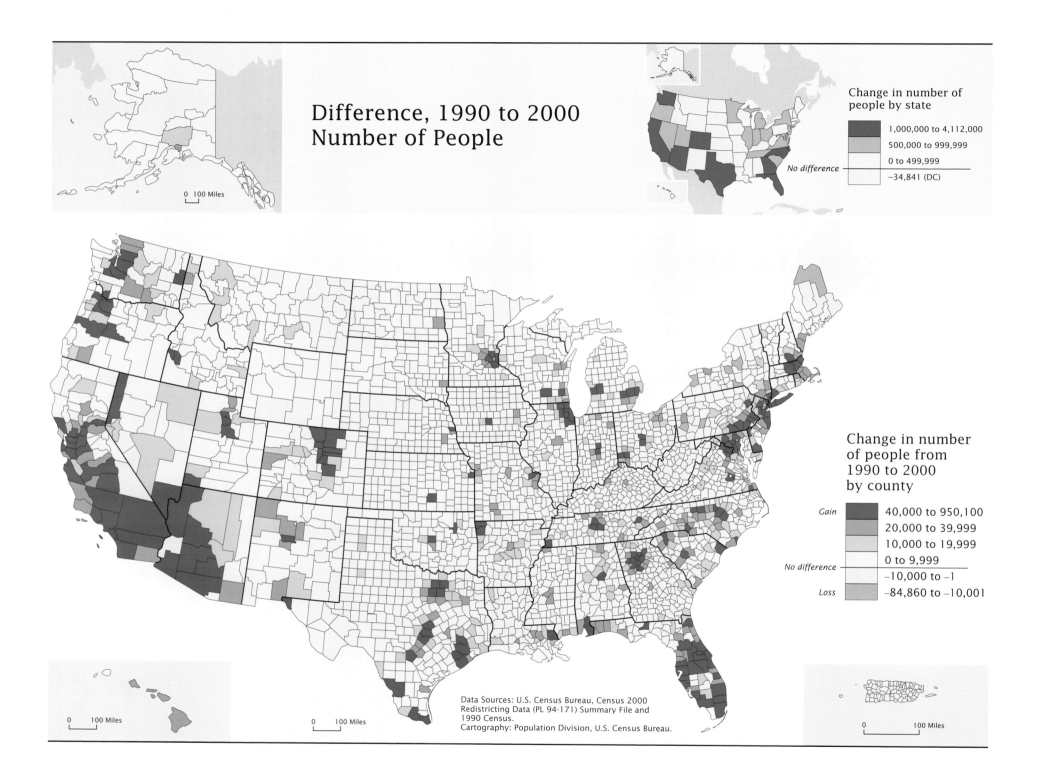

Difference, 1990 to 2000
Number of People

Change in number of
people by state

- 1,000,000 to 4,112,000
- 500,000 to 999,999
- 0 to 499,999
- No difference ———
- −34,841 (DC)

Change in number
of people from
1990 to 2000
by county

Gain
- 40,000 to 950,100
- 20,000 to 39,999
- 10,000 to 19,999
- 0 to 9,999

No difference ———
- −10,000 to −1

Loss
- −84,860 to −10,001

0 100 Miles

0 100 Miles

0 100 Miles

0 100 Miles

Data Sources: U.S. Census Bureau, Census 2000
Redistricting Data (PL 94-171) Summary File and
1990 Census.
Cartography: Population Division, U.S. Census Bureau.

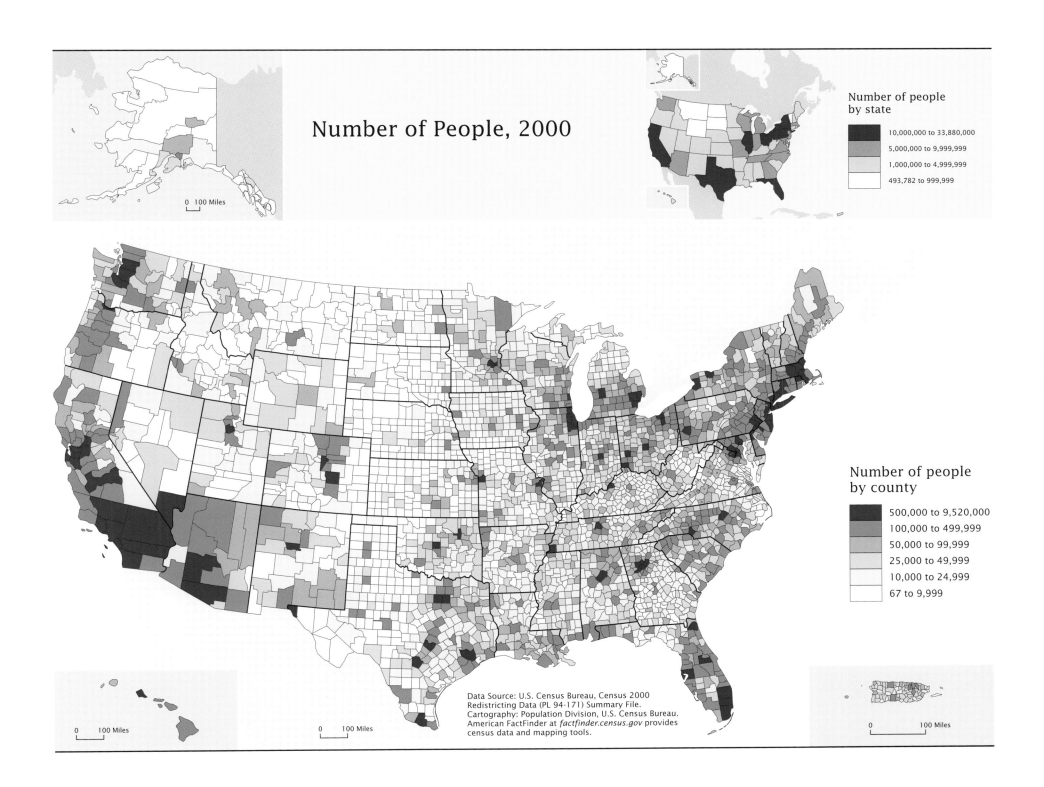

Number of People, 2000

Number of people by state

- 10,000,000 to 33,880,000
- 5,000,000 to 9,999,999
- 1,000,000 to 4,999,999
- 493,782 to 999,999

Number of people by county

- 500,000 to 9,520,000
- 100,000 to 499,999
- 50,000 to 99,999
- 25,000 to 49,999
- 10,000 to 24,999
- 67 to 9,999

0 100 Miles

Data Source: U.S. Census Bureau, Census 2000 Redistricting Data (PL 94-171) Summary File. Cartography: Population Division, U.S. Census Bureau. American FactFinder at *factfinder.census.gov* provides census data and mapping tools.

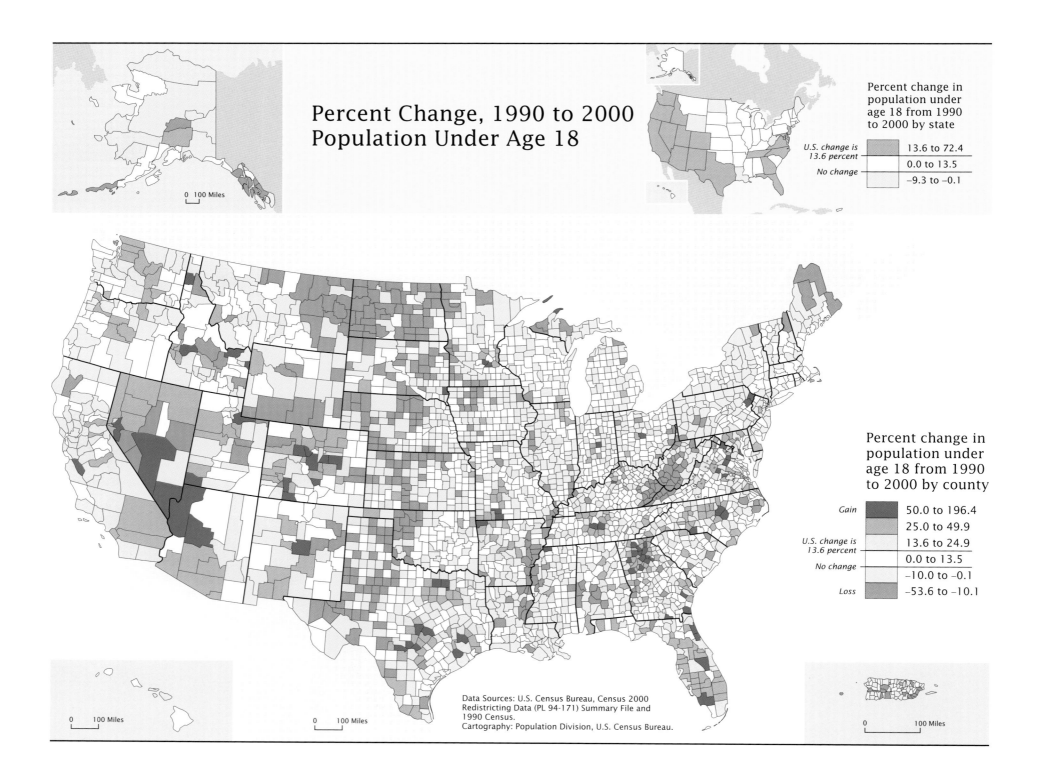

Percent Change, 1990 to 2000
Population Under Age 18

Percent change in
population under
age 18 from 1990
to 2000 by state

U.S. change is
13.6 percent

No change

	13.6 to 72.4
	0.0 to 13.5
	−9.3 to −0.1

Percent change in
population under
age 18 from 1990
to 2000 by county

Gain

U.S. change is
13.6 percent

No change

Loss

	50.0 to 196.4
	25.0 to 49.9
	13.6 to 24.9
	0.0 to 13.5
	−10.0 to −0.1
	−53.6 to −10.1

0 100 Miles

0 100 Miles

0 100 Miles

0 100 Miles

Data Sources: U.S. Census Bureau, Census 2000
Redistricting Data (PL 94-171) Summary File and
1990 Census.
Cartography: Population Division, U.S. Census Bureau.

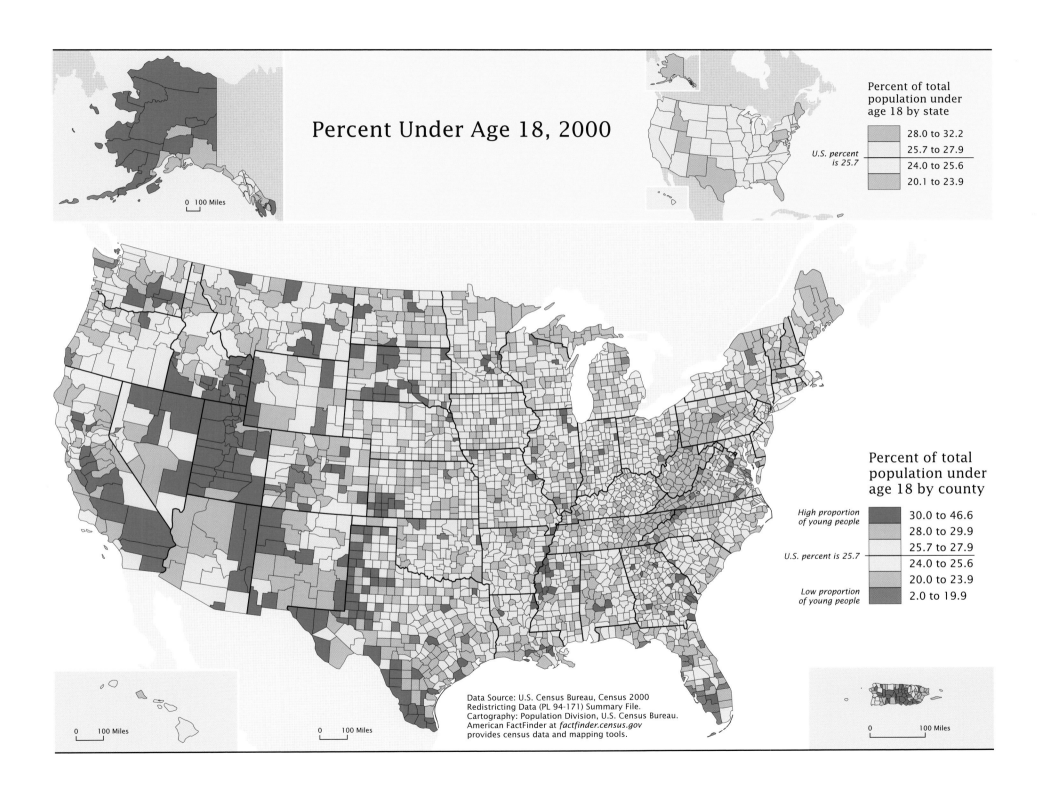

Percent Under Age 18, 2000

Percent of total
population under
age 18 by state

*U.S. percent
is 25.7*

| | 28.0 to 32.2 |
| 25.7 to 27.9 |
| 24.0 to 25.6 |
| 20.1 to 23.9 |

0 100 Miles

Percent of total
population under
age 18 by county

*High proportion
of young people*

U.S. percent is 25.7

*Low proportion
of young people*

| 30.0 to 46.6 |
| 28.0 to 29.9 |
| 25.7 to 27.9 |
| 24.0 to 25.6 |
| 20.0 to 23.9 |
| 2.0 to 19.9 |

0 100 Miles

Data Source: U.S. Census Bureau, Census 2000
Redistricting Data (PL 94-171) Summary File.
Cartography: Population Division, U.S. Census Bureau.
American FactFinder at *factfinder.census.gov*
provides census data and mapping tools.

0 100 Miles

Diversity

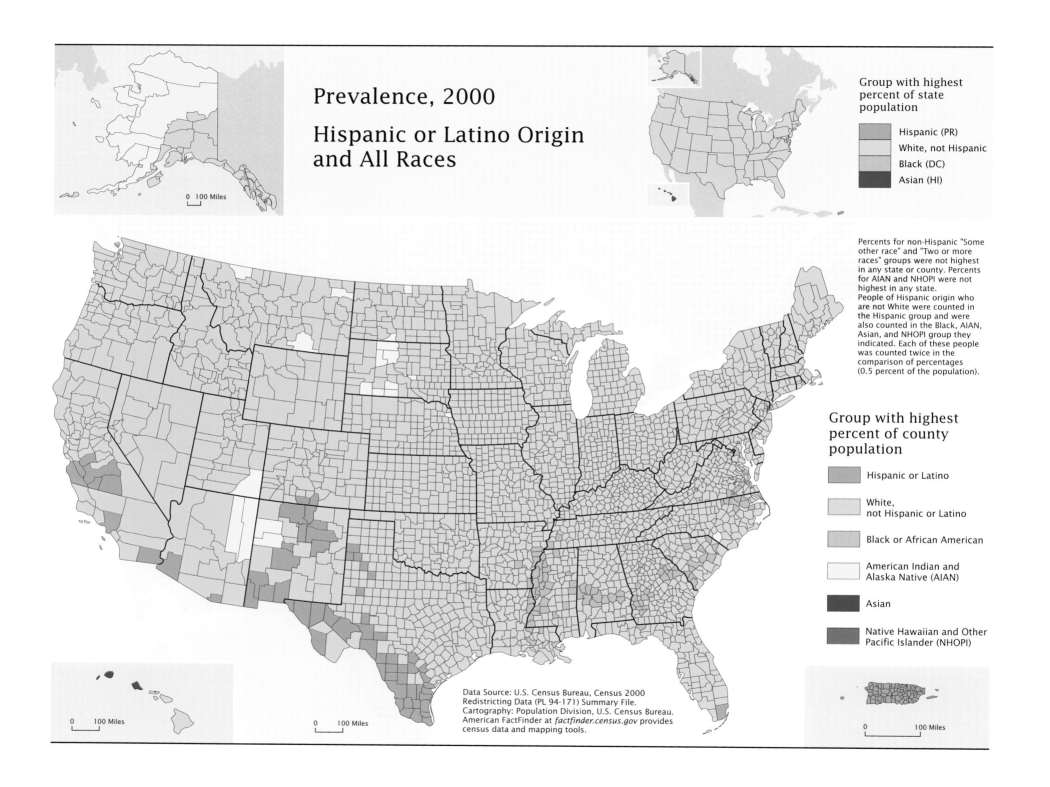

Prevalence, 2000

Hispanic or Latino Origin and All Races

Group with highest percent of state population

- Hispanic (PR)
- White, not Hispanic
- Black (DC)
- Asian (HI)

Percents for non-Hispanic "Some other race" and "Two or more races" groups were not highest in any state or county. Percents for AIAN and NHOPI were not highest in any state.
People of Hispanic origin who are not White were counted in the Hispanic group and were also counted in the Black, AIAN, Asian, and NHOPI group they indicated. Each of these people was counted twice in the comparison of percentages (0.5 percent of the population).

Group with highest percent of county population

- Hispanic or Latino
- White, not Hispanic or Latino
- Black or African American
- American Indian and Alaska Native (AIAN)
- Asian
- Native Hawaiian and Other Pacific Islander (NHOPI)

0 100 Miles

Data Source: U.S. Census Bureau, Census 2000 Redistricting Data (PL 94-171) Summary File.
Cartography: Population Division, U.S. Census Bureau.
American FactFinder at *factfinder.census.gov* provides census data and mapping tools.

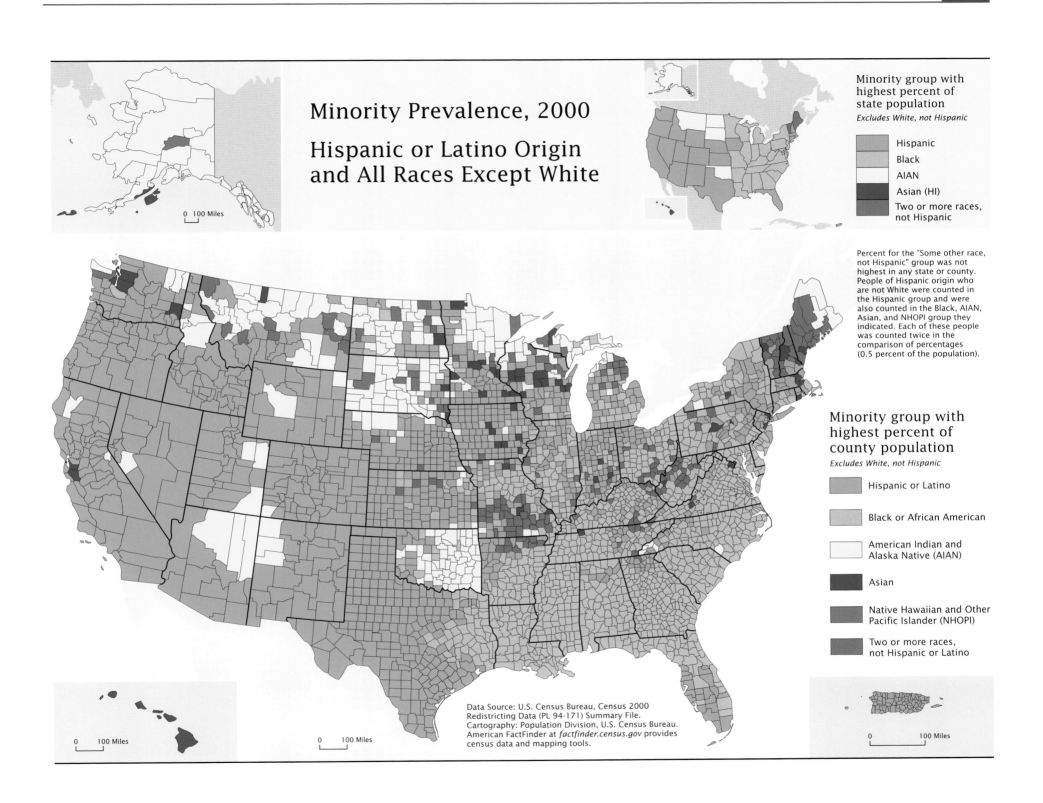

Minority Prevalence, 2000

Hispanic or Latino Origin and All Races Except White

Minority group with highest percent of state population
Excludes White, not Hispanic

- Hispanic
- Black
- AIAN
- Asian (HI)
- Two or more races, not Hispanic

Percent for the "Some other race, not Hispanic" group was not highest in any state or county. People of Hispanic origin who are not White were counted in the Hispanic group and were also counted in the Black, AIAN, Asian, and NHOPI group they indicated. Each of these people was counted twice in the comparison of percentages (0.5 percent of the population).

Minority group with highest percent of county population
Excludes White, not Hispanic

- Hispanic or Latino
- Black or African American
- American Indian and Alaska Native (AIAN)
- Asian
- Native Hawaiian and Other Pacific Islander (NHOPI)
- Two or more races, not Hispanic or Latino

Data Source: U.S. Census Bureau, Census 2000 Redistricting Data (PL 94-171) Summary File.
Cartography: Population Division, U.S. Census Bureau. American FactFinder at *factfinder.census.gov* provides census data and mapping tools.

0 100 Miles

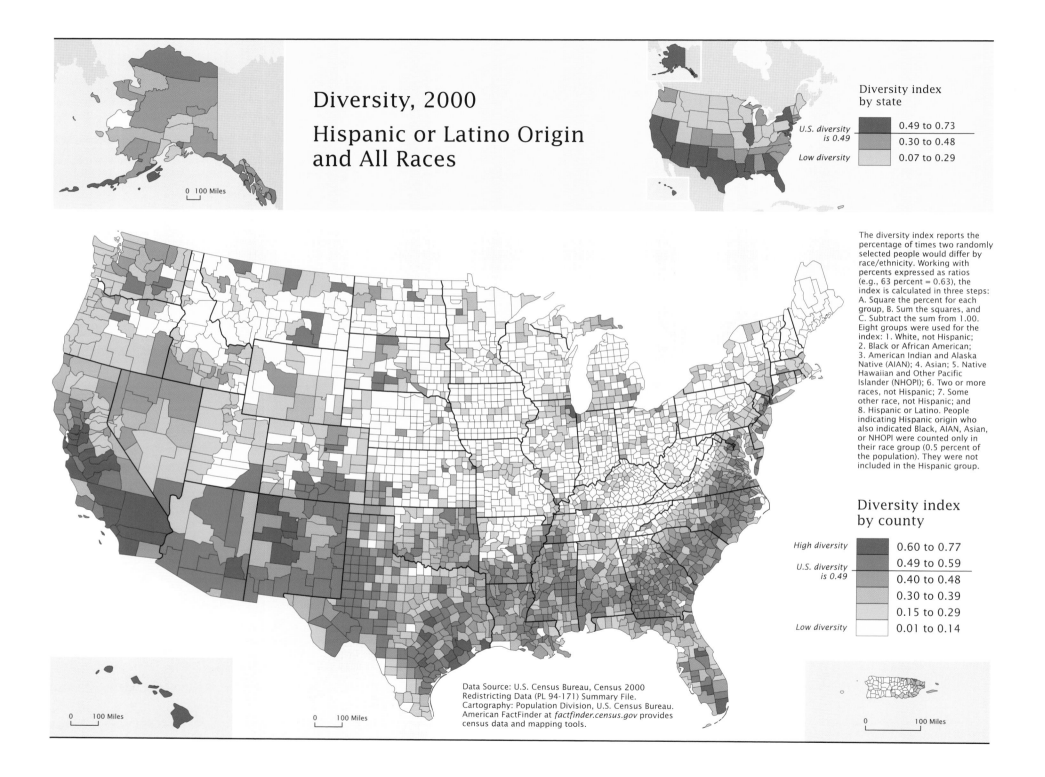

Diversity, 2000

Hispanic or Latino Origin and All Races

Diversity index by state

U.S. diversity is 0.49

	0.49 to 0.73
	0.30 to 0.48
Low diversity	0.07 to 0.29

The diversity index reports the percentage of times two randomly selected people would differ by race/ethnicity. Working with percents expressed as ratios (e.g., 63 percent = 0.63), the index is calculated in three steps: A. Square the percent for each group, B. Sum the squares, and C. Subtract the sum from 1.00. Eight groups were used for the index: 1. White, not Hispanic; 2. Black or African American; 3. American Indian and Alaska Native (AIAN); 4. Asian; 5. Native Hawaiian and Other Pacific Islander (NHOPI); 6. Two or more races, not Hispanic; 7. Some other race, not Hispanic; and 8. Hispanic or Latino. People indicating Hispanic origin who also indicated Black, AIAN, Asian, or NHOPI were counted only in their race group (0.5 percent of the population). They were not included in the Hispanic group.

Diversity index by county

High diversity	0.60 to 0.77
U.S. diversity is 0.49	0.49 to 0.59
	0.40 to 0.48
	0.30 to 0.39
	0.15 to 0.29
Low diversity	0.01 to 0.14

Data Source: U.S. Census Bureau, Census 2000 Redistricting Data (PL 94-171) Summary File. Cartography: Population Division, U.S. Census Bureau. American FactFinder at *factfinder.census.gov* provides census data and mapping tools.

0 100 Miles

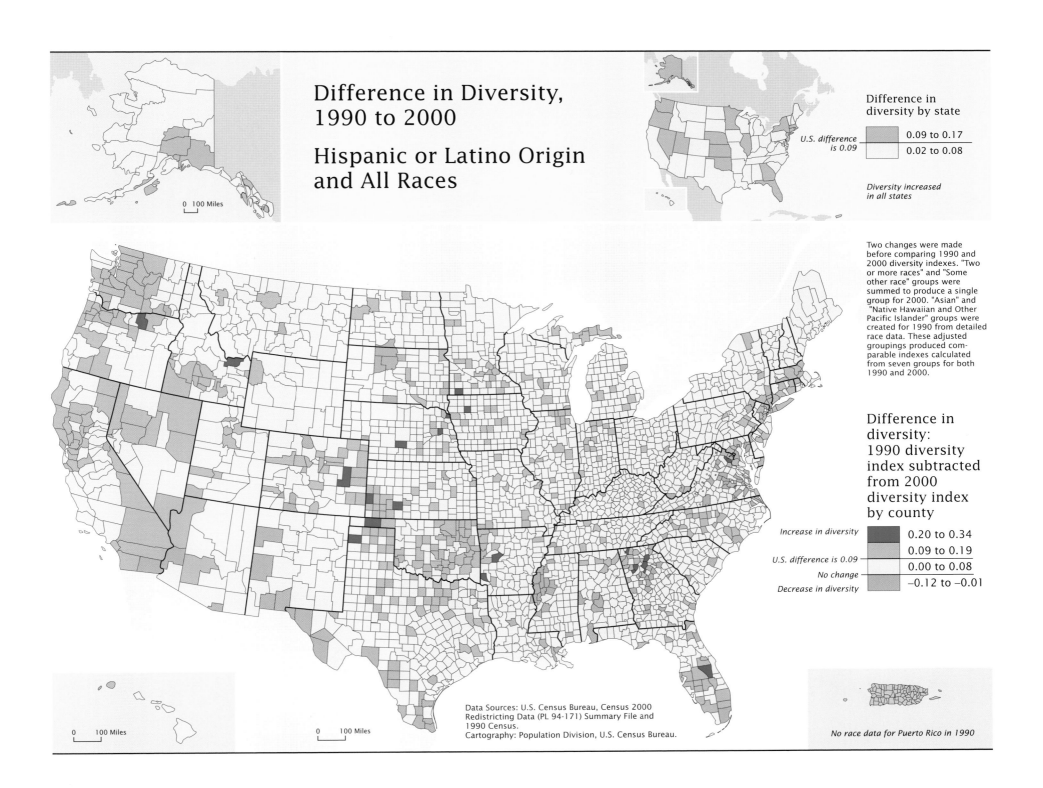

Difference in Diversity, 1990 to 2000

Hispanic or Latino Origin and All Races

Difference in diversity by state

U.S. difference is 0.09

0.09 to 0.17
0.02 to 0.08

Diversity increased in all states

Two changes were made before comparing 1990 and 2000 diversity indexes. "Two or more races" and "Some other race" groups were summed to produce a single group for 2000. "Asian" and "Native Hawaiian and Other Pacific Islander" groups were created for 1990 from detailed race data. These adjusted groupings produced comparable indexes calculated from seven groups for both 1990 and 2000.

Difference in diversity: 1990 diversity index subtracted from 2000 diversity index by county

Increase in diversity
0.20 to 0.34
0.09 to 0.19

U.S. difference is 0.09

0.00 to 0.08

No change
−0.12 to −0.01

Decrease in diversity

0   100 Miles

0   100 Miles

0   100 Miles

Data Sources: U.S. Census Bureau, Census 2000 Redistricting Data (PL 94-171) Summary File and 1990 Census.
Cartography: Population Division, U.S. Census Bureau.

No race data for Puerto Rico in 1990

White

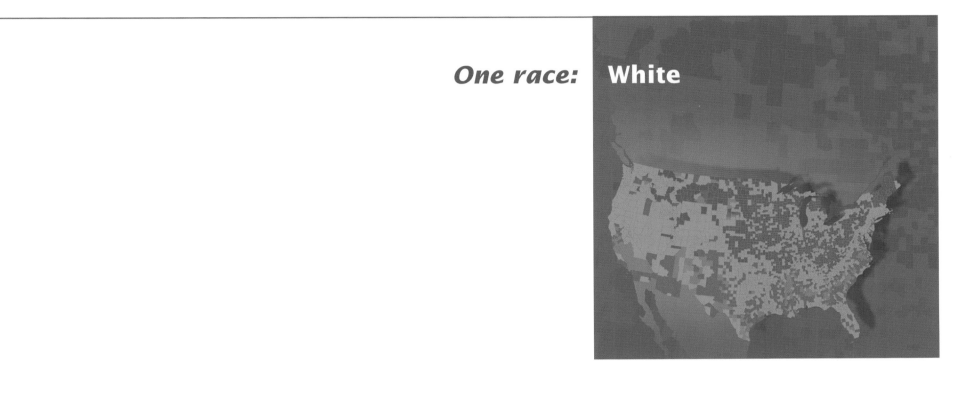

One race: **White**

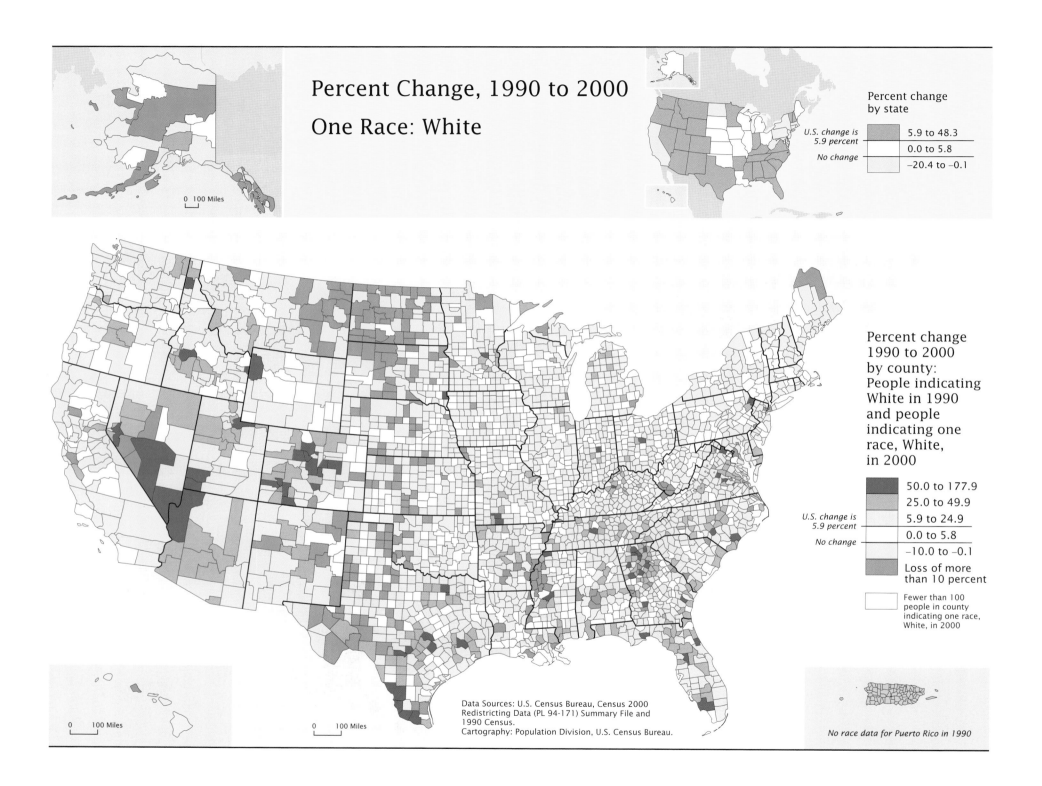

Percent Change, 1990 to 2000

One Race: White

Percent change
by state

*U.S. change is
5.9 percent*

No change

5.9 to 48.3

0.0 to 5.8

−20.4 to −0.1

0 100 Miles

Percent change
1990 to 2000
by county:
People indicating
White in 1990
and people
indicating one
race, White,
in 2000

50.0 to 177.9

25.0 to 49.9

*U.S. change is
5.9 percent* — 5.9 to 24.9

No change — 0.0 to 5.8

−10.0 to −0.1

Loss of more
than 10 percent

Fewer than 100
people in county
indicating one race,
White, in 2000

0 100 Miles

0 100 Miles

Data Sources: U.S. Census Bureau, Census 2000
Redistricting Data (PL 94-171) Summary File and
1990 Census.
Cartography: Population Division, U.S. Census Bureau.

No race data for Puerto Rico in 1990

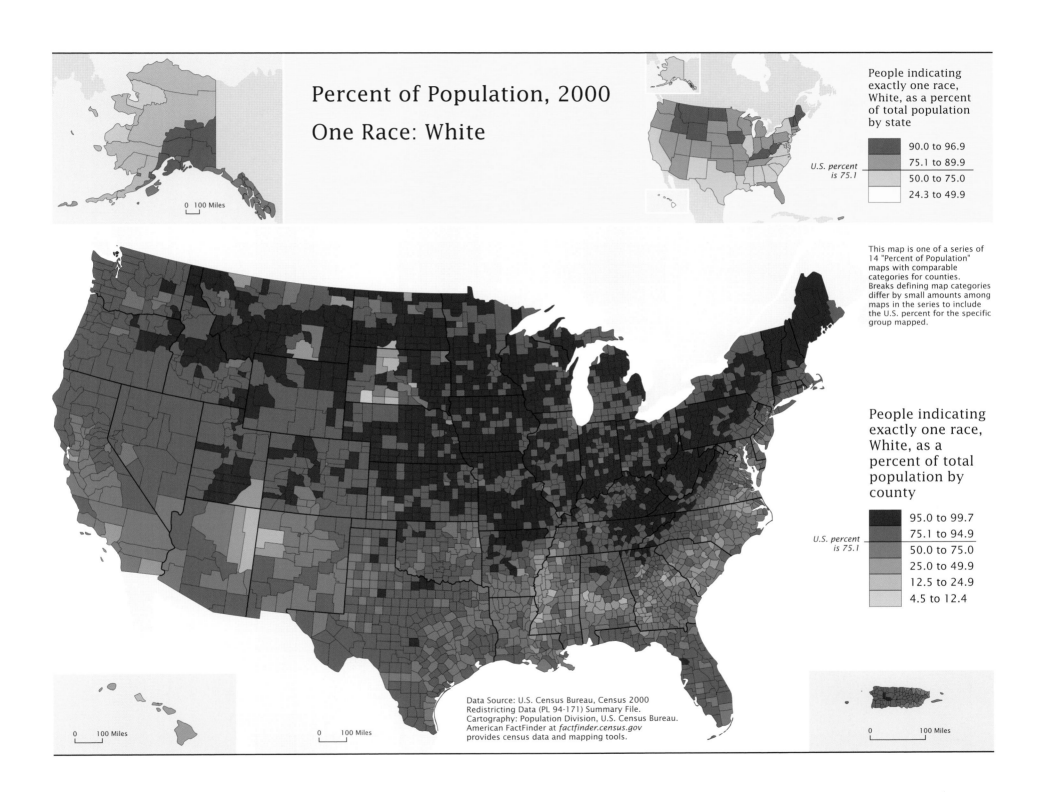

Percent of Population, 2000

One Race: White

People indicating
exactly one race,
White, as a percent
of total population
by state

	90.0 to 96.9
	75.1 to 89.9
	50.0 to 75.0
	24.3 to 49.9

U.S. percent
is 75.1

This map is one of a series of
14 "Percent of Population"
maps with comparable
categories for counties.
Breaks defining map categories
differ by small amounts among
maps in the series to include
the U.S. percent for the specific
group mapped.

People indicating
exactly one race,
White, as a
percent of total
population by
county

	95.0 to 99.7
	75.1 to 94.9
	50.0 to 75.0
	25.0 to 49.9
	12.5 to 24.9
	4.5 to 12.4

U.S. percent
is 75.1

0 100 Miles

0 100 Miles

0 100 Miles

0 100 Miles

Data Source: U.S. Census Bureau, Census 2000
Redistricting Data (PL 94-171) Summary File.
Cartography: Population Division, U.S. Census Bureau.
American FactFinder at *factfinder.census.gov*
provides census data and mapping tools.

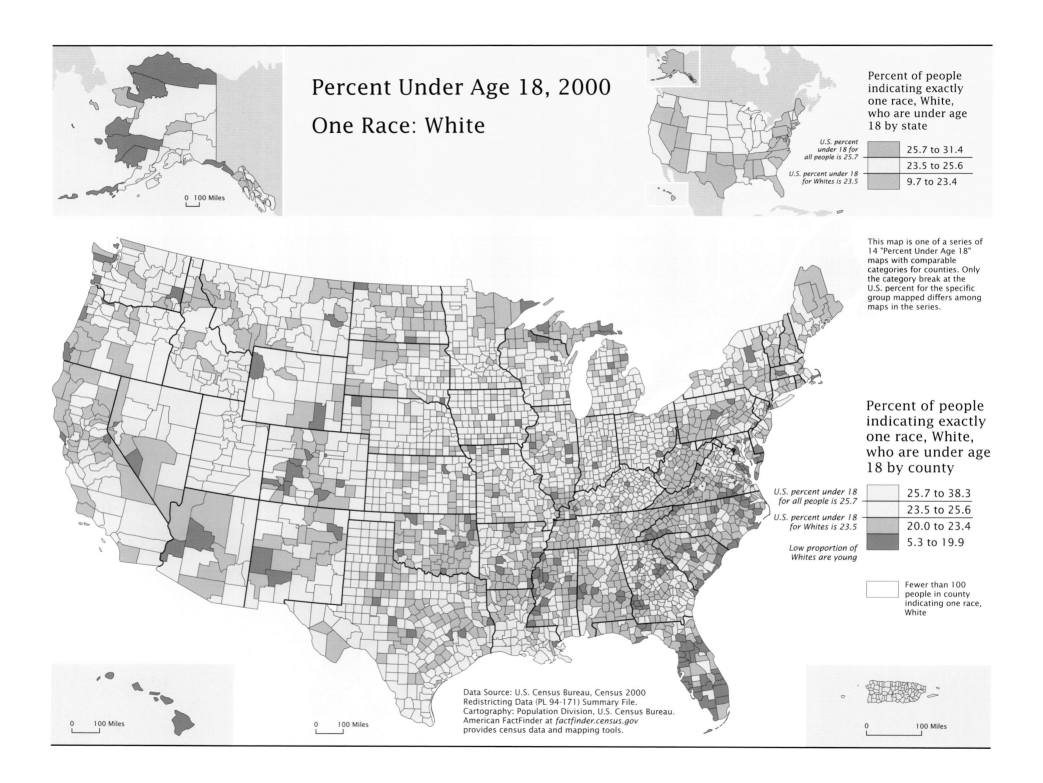

Percent Under Age 18, 2000

One Race: White

Percent of people indicating exactly one race, White, who are under age 18 by state

U.S. percent under 18 for all people is 25.7

U.S. percent under 18 for Whites is 23.5

	25.7 to 31.4
	23.5 to 25.6
	9.7 to 23.4

This map is one of a series of 14 "Percent Under Age 18" maps with comparable categories for counties. Only the category break at the U.S. percent for the specific group mapped differs among maps in the series.

Percent of people indicating exactly one race, White, who are under age 18 by county

U.S. percent under 18 for all people is 25.7

U.S. percent under 18 for Whites is 23.5

	25.7 to 38.3
	23.5 to 25.6
	20.0 to 23.4
	5.3 to 19.9

Low proportion of Whites are young

Fewer than 100 people in county indicating one race, White

0 100 Miles

0 100 Miles

0 100 Miles

Data Source: U.S. Census Bureau, Census 2000 Redistricting Data (PL 94-171) Summary File. Cartography: Population Division, U.S. Census Bureau. American FactFinder at *factfinder.census.gov* provides census data and mapping tools.

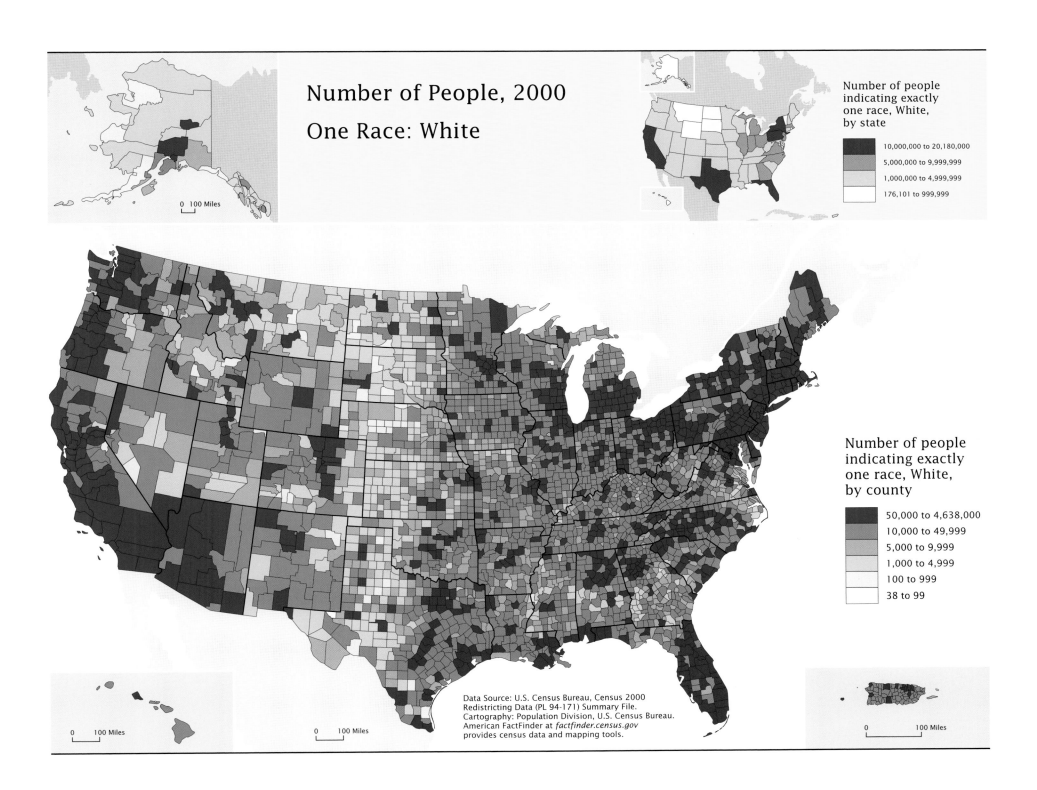

Number of People, 2000

One Race: White

Number of people indicating exactly one race, White, by state

- 10,000,000 to 20,180,000
- 5,000,000 to 9,999,999
- 1,000,000 to 4,999,999
- 176,101 to 999,999

Number of people indicating exactly one race, White, by county

- 50,000 to 4,638,000
- 10,000 to 49,999
- 5,000 to 9,999
- 1,000 to 4,999
- 100 to 999
- 38 to 99

0 100 Miles

Data Source: U.S. Census Bureau, Census 2000
Redistricting Data (PL 94-171) Summary File.
Cartography: Population Division, U.S. Census Bureau.
American FactFinder at *factfinder.census.gov*
provides census data and mapping tools.

0 100 Miles

0 100 Miles

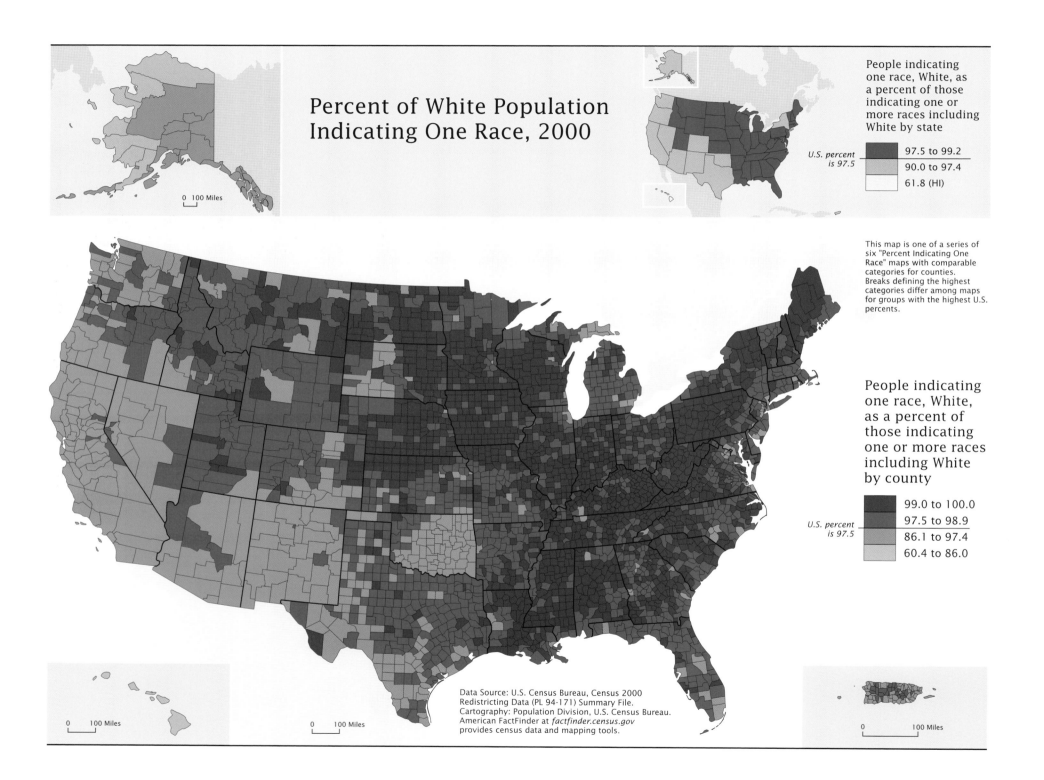

Percent of White Population Indicating One Race, 2000

People indicating one race, White, as a percent of those indicating one or more races including White by state

U.S. percent is 97.5

	97.5 to 99.2
	90.0 to 97.4
	61.8 (HI)

This map is one of a series of six "Percent Indicating One Race" maps with comparable categories for counties. Breaks defining the highest categories differ among maps for groups with the highest U.S. percents.

People indicating one race, White, as a percent of those indicating one or more races including White by county

U.S. percent is 97.5

	99.0 to 100.0
	97.5 to 98.9
	86.1 to 97.4
	60.4 to 86.0

Data Source: U.S. Census Bureau, Census 2000 Redistricting Data (PL 94-171) Summary File. Cartography: Population Division, U.S. Census Bureau. American FactFinder at *factfinder.census.gov* provides census data and mapping tools.

0 100 Miles

0 100 Miles

0 100 Miles

0 100 Miles

White

One or more races including **White**

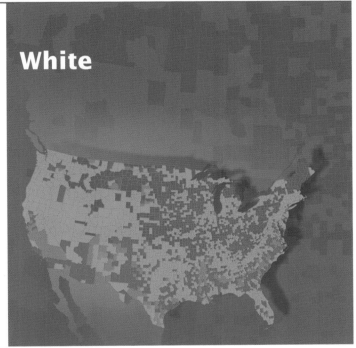

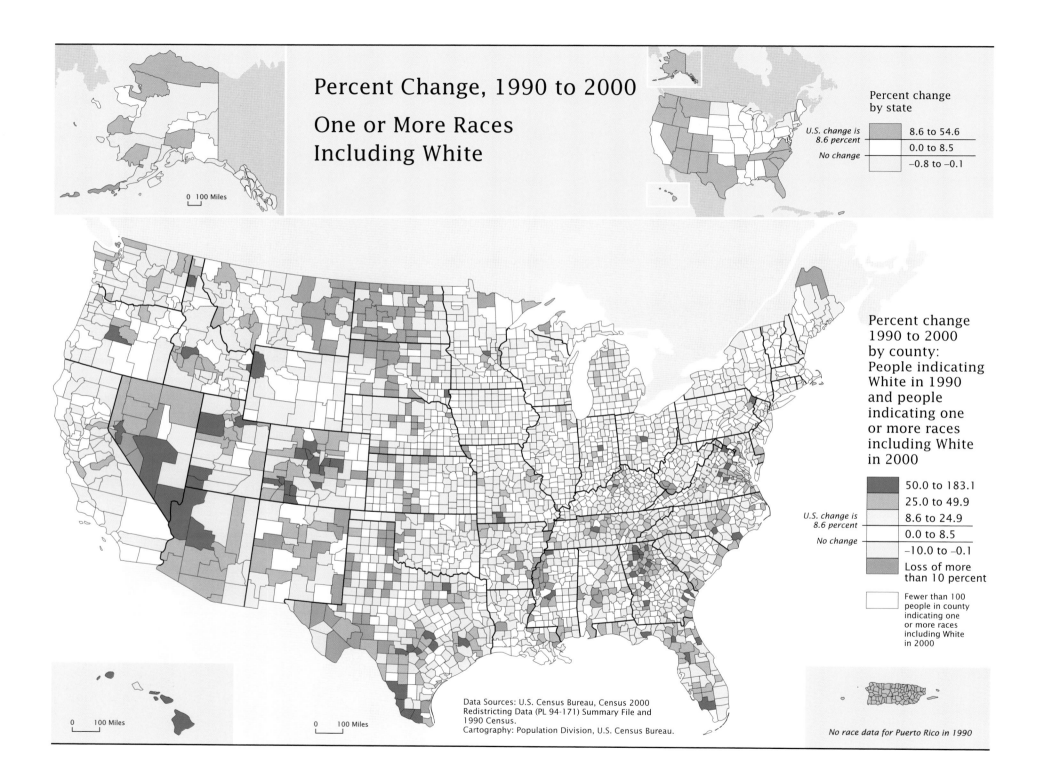

Percent Change, 1990 to 2000

One or More Races
Including White

0 100 Miles

Percent change
by state

U.S. change is
8.6 percent

No change

	8.6 to 54.6
	0.0 to 8.5
	−0.8 to −0.1

Percent change
1990 to 2000
by county:
People indicating
White in 1990
and people
indicating one
or more races
including White
in 2000

U.S. change is
8.6 percent

No change

	50.0 to 183.1
	25.0 to 49.9
	8.6 to 24.9
	0.0 to 8.5
	−10.0 to −0.1
	Loss of more than 10 percent
	Fewer than 100 people in county indicating one or more races including White in 2000

Data Sources: U.S. Census Bureau, Census 2000
Redistricting Data (PL 94-171) Summary File and
1990 Census.
Cartography: Population Division, U.S. Census Bureau.

0 100 Miles

0 100 Miles

No race data for Puerto Rico in 1990

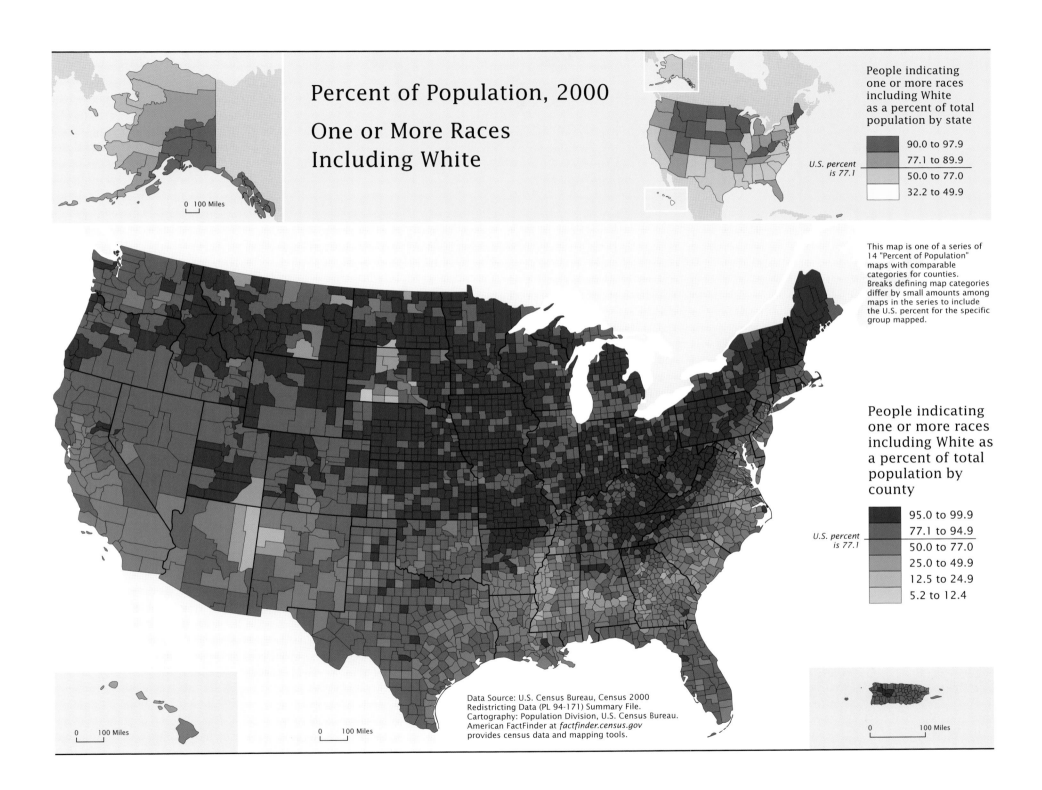

Percent of Population, 2000

One or More Races
Including White

People indicating
one or more races
including White
as a percent of total
population by state

*U.S. percent
is 77.1*

90.0 to 97.9
77.1 to 89.9
50.0 to 77.0
32.2 to 49.9

This map is one of a series of
14 "Percent of Population"
maps with comparable
categories for counties.
Breaks defining map categories
differ by small amounts among
maps in the series to include
the U.S. percent for the specific
group mapped.

People indicating
one or more races
including White as
a percent of total
population by
county

*U.S. percent
is 77.1*

95.0 to 99.9
77.1 to 94.9
50.0 to 77.0
25.0 to 49.9
12.5 to 24.9
5.2 to 12.4

0 100 Miles

Data Source: U.S. Census Bureau, Census 2000
Redistricting Data (PL 94-171) Summary File.
Cartography: Population Division, U.S. Census Bureau.
American FactFinder at *factfinder.census.gov*
provides census data and mapping tools.

0 100 Miles   0 100 Miles   0 100 Miles

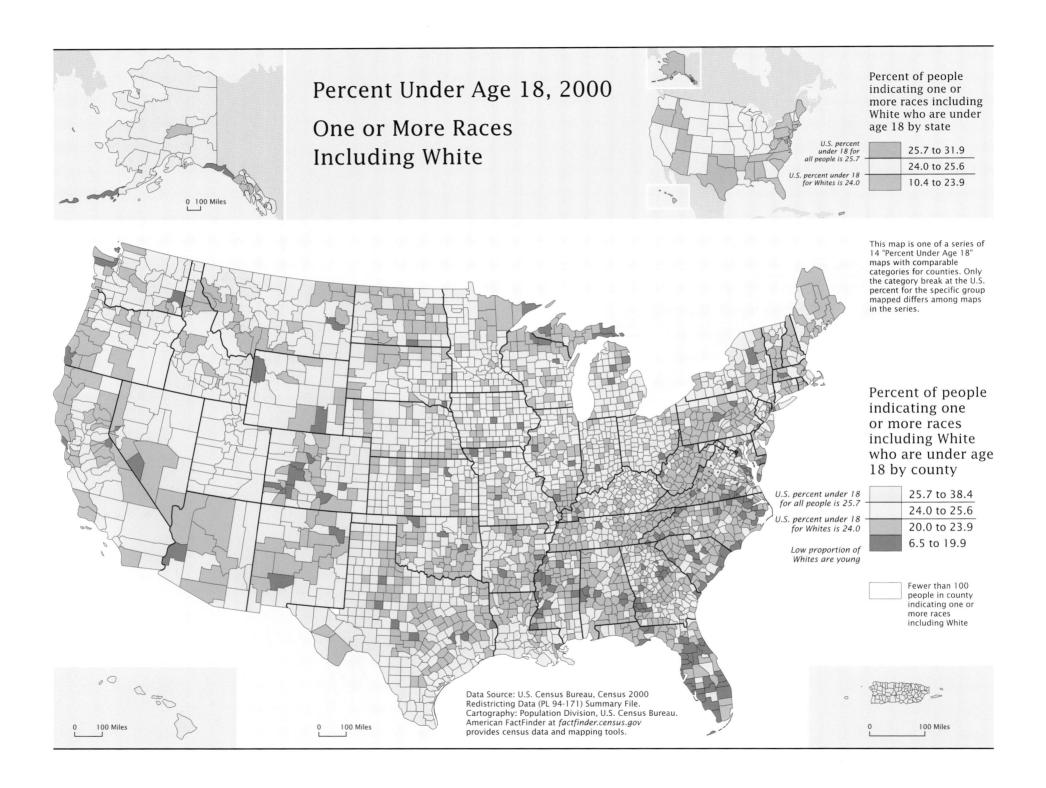

Percent Under Age 18, 2000

One or More Races Including White

Percent of people indicating one or more races including White who are under age 18 by state

U.S. percent under 18 for all people is 25.7
U.S. percent under 18 for Whites is 24.0

25.7 to 31.9
24.0 to 25.6
10.4 to 23.9

This map is one of a series of 14 "Percent Under Age 18" maps with comparable categories for counties. Only the category break at the U.S. percent for the specific group mapped differs among maps in the series.

Percent of people indicating one or more races including White who are under age 18 by county

U.S. percent under 18 for all people is 25.7
U.S. percent under 18 for Whites is 24.0
Low proportion of Whites are young

25.7 to 38.4
24.0 to 25.6
20.0 to 23.9
6.5 to 19.9

Fewer than 100 people in county indicating one or more races including White

Data Source: U.S. Census Bureau, Census 2000 Redistricting Data (PL 94-171) Summary File.
Cartography: Population Division, U.S. Census Bureau.
American FactFinder at *factfinder.census.gov* provides census data and mapping tools.

0 100 Miles

0 100 Miles

0 100 Miles

0 100 Miles

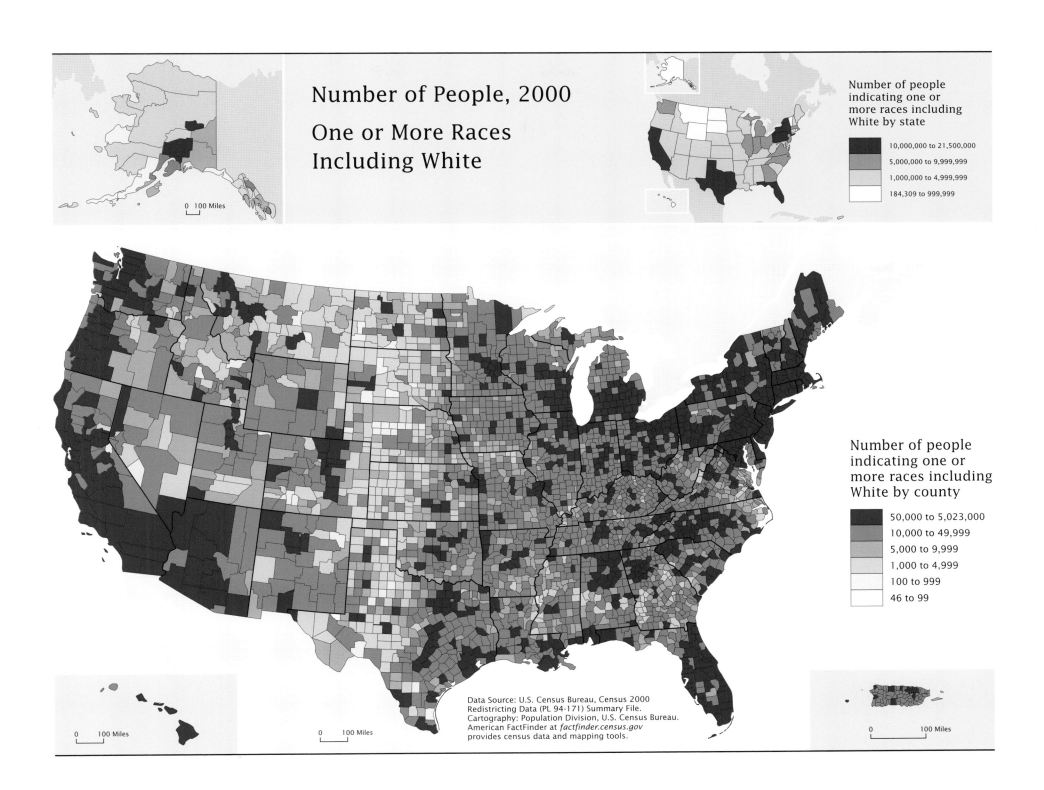

Number of People, 2000

One or More Races
Including White

0 100 Miles

Number of people
indicating one or
more races including
White by state

10,000,000 to 21,500,000
5,000,000 to 9,999,999
1,000,000 to 4,999,999
184,309 to 999,999

Number of people
indicating one or
more races including
White by county

50,000 to 5,023,000
10,000 to 49,999
5,000 to 9,999
1,000 to 4,999
100 to 999
46 to 99

Data Source: U.S. Census Bureau, Census 2000
Redistricting Data (PL 94-171) Summary File.
Cartography: Population Division, U.S. Census Bureau.
American FactFinder at *factfinder.census.gov*
provides census data and mapping tools.

0 100 Miles

0 100 Miles

0 100 Miles

Black or African American

One race: **Black or African American**

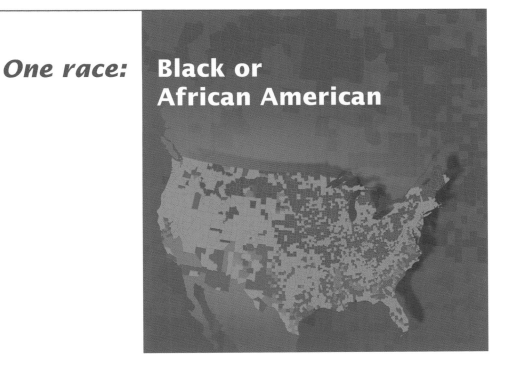

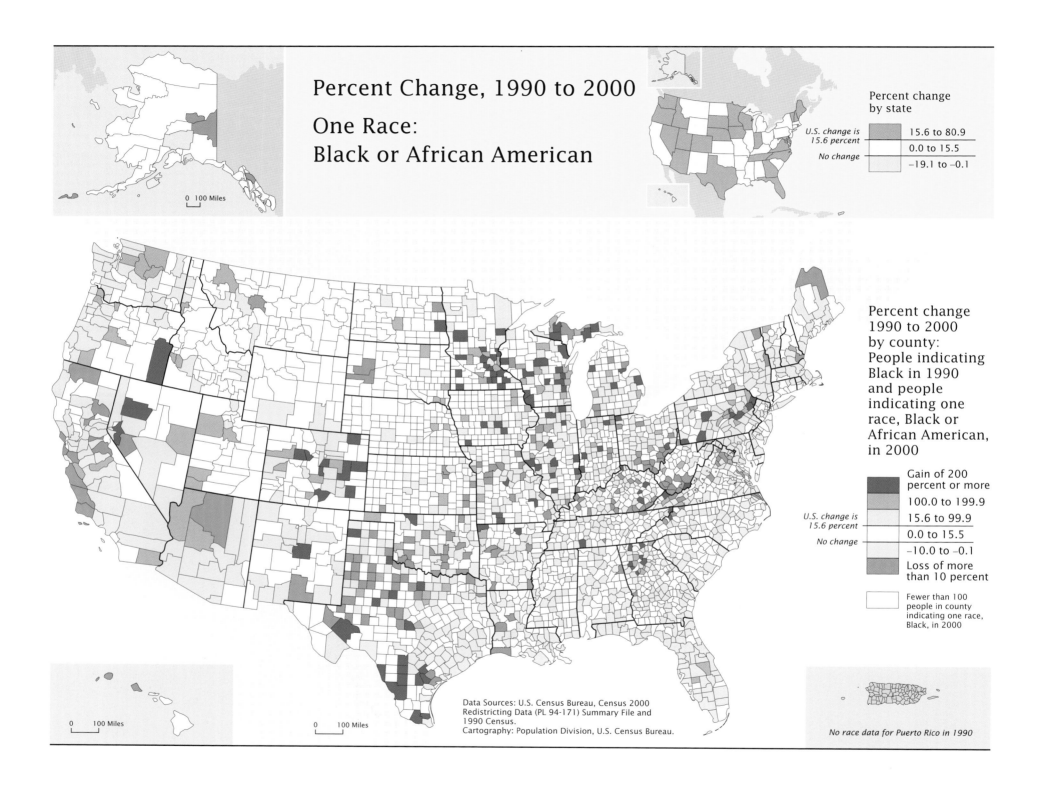

Percent Change, 1990 to 2000

One Race:
Black or African American

Percent change
by state

U.S. change is
15.6 percent

| | 15.6 to 80.9 |
| | 0.0 to 15.5 |
No change | | −19.1 to −0.1 |

Percent change
1990 to 2000
by county:
People indicating
Black in 1990
and people
indicating one
race, Black or
African American,
in 2000

Gain of 200
percent or more

100.0 to 199.9

U.S. change is
15.6 percent — 15.6 to 99.9

0.0 to 15.5

No change — −10.0 to −0.1

Loss of more
than 10 percent

Fewer than 100
people in county
indicating one race,
Black, in 2000

0   100 Miles

0   100 Miles

Data Sources: U.S. Census Bureau, Census 2000
Redistricting Data (PL 94-171) Summary File and
1990 Census.
Cartography: Population Division, U.S. Census Bureau.

No race data for Puerto Rico in 1990

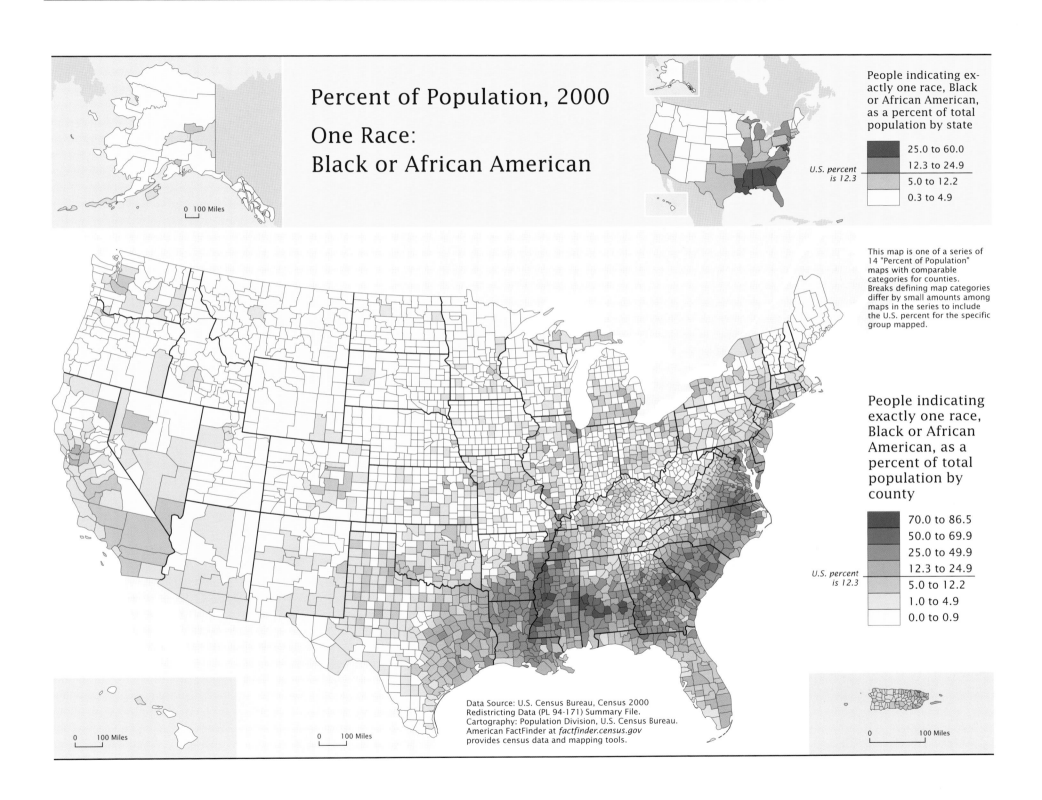

Percent of Population, 2000

One Race:
Black or African American

People indicating exactly one race, Black or African American, as a percent of total population by state

	25.0 to 60.0
	12.3 to 24.9
	5.0 to 12.2
	0.3 to 4.9

U.S. percent is 12.3

This map is one of a series of 14 "Percent of Population" maps with comparable categories for counties. Breaks defining map categories differ by small amounts among maps in the series to include the U.S. percent for the specific group mapped.

People indicating exactly one race, Black or African American, as a percent of total population by county

	70.0 to 86.5
	50.0 to 69.9
	25.0 to 49.9
	12.3 to 24.9
	5.0 to 12.2
	1.0 to 4.9
	0.0 to 0.9

U.S. percent is 12.3

Data Source: U.S. Census Bureau, Census 2000 Redistricting Data (PL 94-171) Summary File.
Cartography: Population Division, U.S. Census Bureau.
American FactFinder at *factfinder.census.gov* provides census data and mapping tools.

0   100 Miles

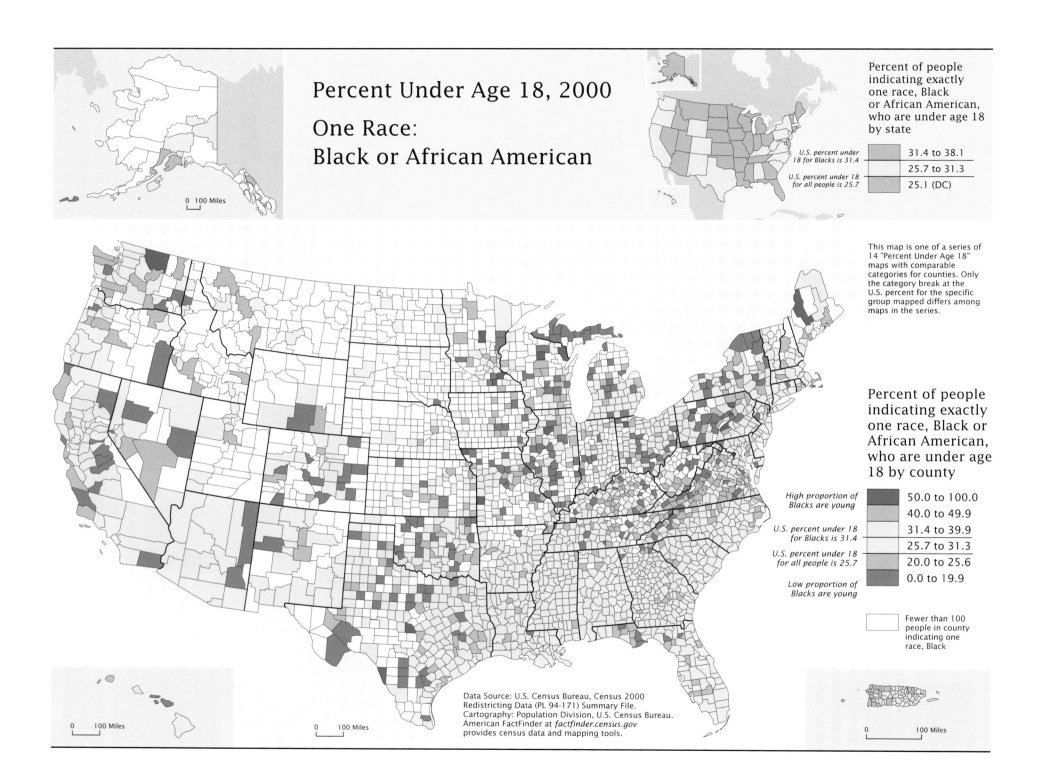

Percent Under Age 18, 2000

One Race:

Black or African American

Percent of people indicating exactly one race, Black or African American, who are under age 18 by state

U.S. percent under 18 for Blacks is 31.4
U.S. percent under 18 for all people is 25.7

	31.4 to 38.1
	25.7 to 31.3
	25.1 (DC)

This map is one of a series of 14 "Percent Under Age 18" maps with comparable categories for counties. Only the category break at the U.S. percent for the specific group mapped differs among maps in the series.

Percent of people indicating exactly one race, Black or African American, who are under age 18 by county

High proportion of Blacks are young

U.S. percent under 18 for Blacks is 31.4

U.S. percent under 18 for all people is 25.7

Low proportion of Blacks are young

	50.0 to 100.0
	40.0 to 49.9
	31.4 to 39.9
	25.7 to 31.3
	20.0 to 25.6
	0.0 to 19.9

Fewer than 100 people in county indicating one race, Black

0 100 Miles

0 100 Miles

0 100 Miles

0 100 Miles

Data Source: U.S. Census Bureau, Census 2000 Redistricting Data (PL 94-171) Summary File. Cartography: Population Division, U.S. Census Bureau. American FactFinder at *factfinder.census.gov* provides census data and mapping tools.

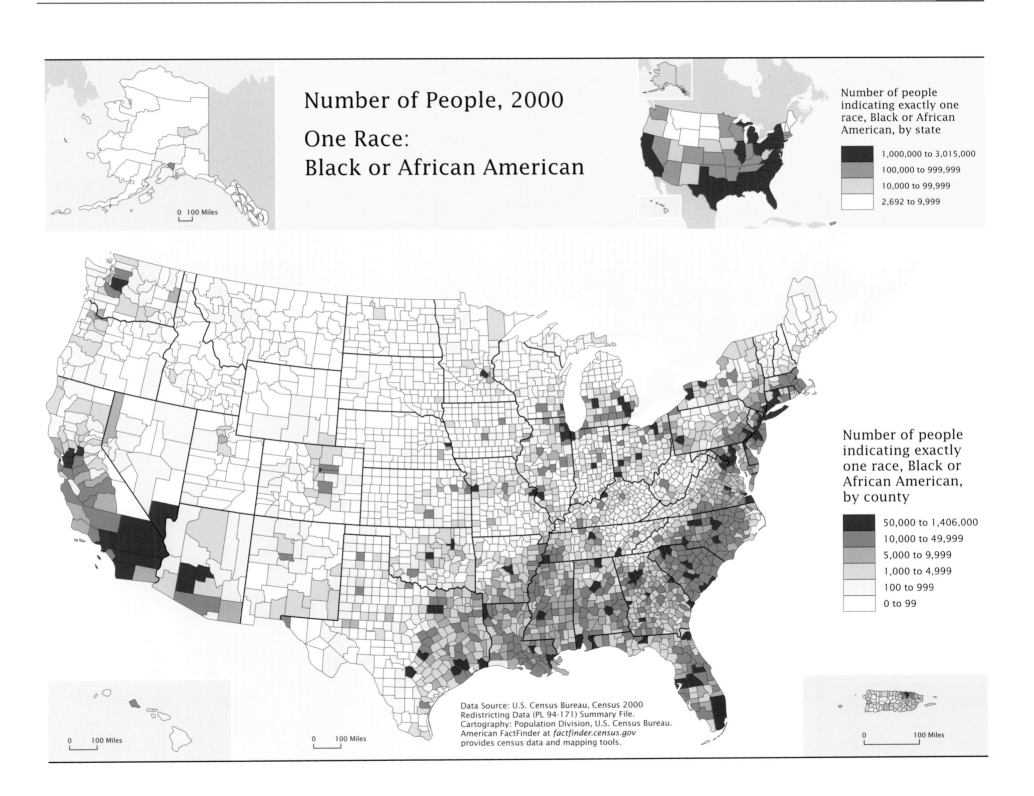

Number of People, 2000

One Race:
Black or African American

Number of people indicating exactly one race, Black or African American, by state

1,000,000 to 3,015,000
100,000 to 999,999
10,000 to 99,999
2,692 to 9,999

Number of people indicating exactly one race, Black or African American, by county

50,000 to 1,406,000
10,000 to 49,999
5,000 to 9,999
1,000 to 4,999
100 to 999
0 to 99

0 100 Miles

Data Source: U.S. Census Bureau, Census 2000
Redistricting Data (PL 94-171) Summary File.
Cartography: Population Division, U.S. Census Bureau.
American FactFinder at *factfinder.census.gov*
provides census data and mapping tools.

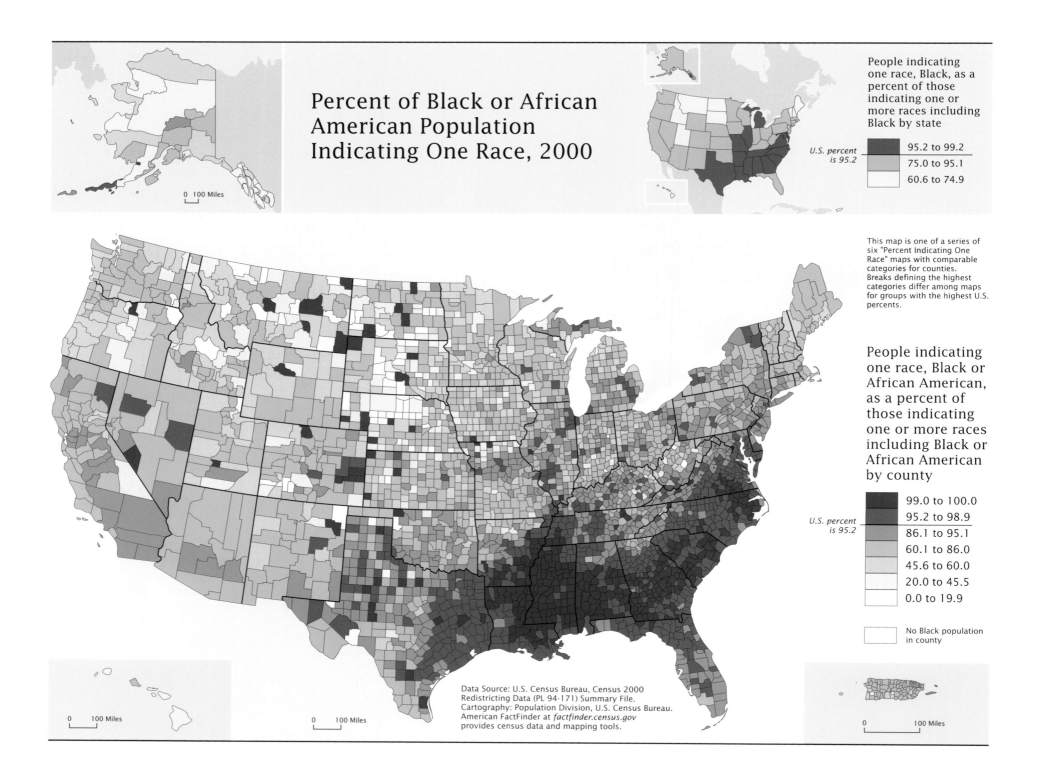

Percent of Black or African American Population Indicating One Race, 2000

People indicating one race, Black, as a percent of those indicating one or more races including Black by state

U.S. percent is 95.2

	95.2 to 99.2
	75.0 to 95.1
	60.6 to 74.9

This map is one of a series of six "Percent Indicating One Race" maps with comparable categories for counties. Breaks defining the highest categories differ among maps for groups with the highest U.S. percents.

People indicating one race, Black or African American, as a percent of those indicating one or more races including Black or African American by county

U.S. percent is 95.2

	99.0 to 100.0
	95.2 to 98.9
	86.1 to 95.1
	60.1 to 86.0
	45.6 to 60.0
	20.0 to 45.5
	0.0 to 19.9

	No Black population in county

0 100 Miles

Data Source: U.S. Census Bureau, Census 2000 Redistricting Data (PL 94-171) Summary File. Cartography: Population Division, U.S. Census Bureau. American FactFinder at *factfinder.census.gov* provides census data and mapping tools.

0 100 Miles

0 100 Miles

0 100 Miles

Black or African American

One or more races including **Black or African American**

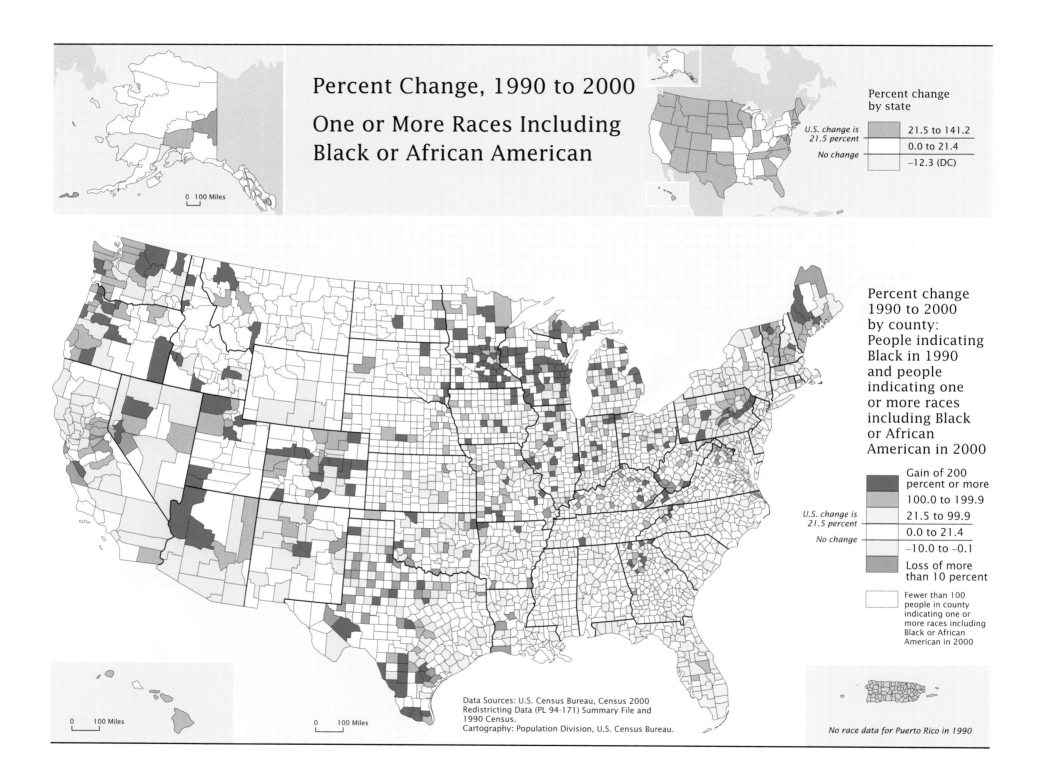

Percent Change, 1990 to 2000

One or More Races Including Black or African American

Percent change by state

U.S. change is 21.5 percent

No change

	21.5 to 141.2
	0.0 to 21.4
	−12.3 (DC)

Percent change 1990 to 2000 by county: People indicating Black in 1990 and people indicating one or more races including Black or African American in 2000

U.S. change is 21.5 percent

No change

Gain of 200 percent or more
100.0 to 199.9
21.5 to 99.9
0.0 to 21.4
−10.0 to −0.1
Loss of more than 10 percent

Fewer than 100 people in county indicating one or more races including Black or African American in 2000

0 100 Miles

0 100 Miles

Data Sources: U.S. Census Bureau, Census 2000 Redistricting Data (PL 94-171) Summary File and 1990 Census.
Cartography: Population Division, U.S. Census Bureau.

No race data for Puerto Rico in 1990

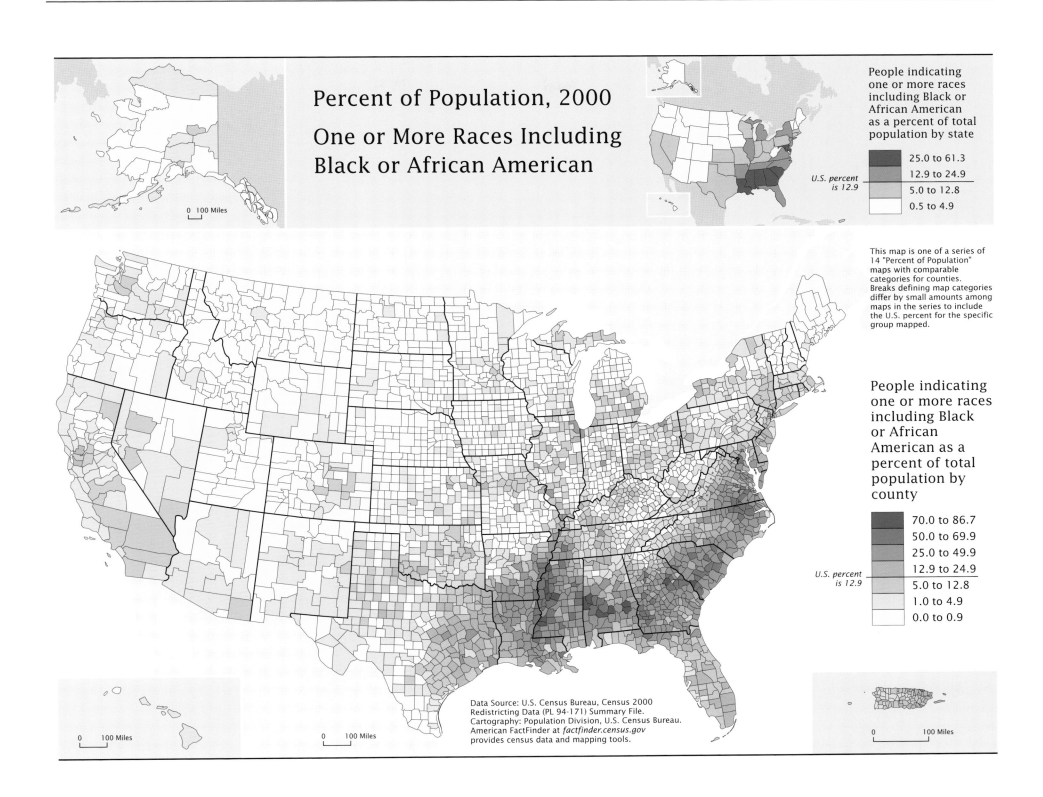

Percent of Population, 2000

One or More Races Including Black or African American

People indicating one or more races including Black or African American as a percent of total population by state

25.0 to 61.3
12.9 to 24.9
5.0 to 12.8
0.5 to 4.9

U.S. percent is 12.9

0   100 Miles

This map is one of a series of 14 "Percent of Population" maps with comparable categories for counties. Breaks defining map categories differ by small amounts among maps in the series to include the U.S. percent for the specific group mapped.

People indicating one or more races including Black or African American as a percent of total population by county

70.0 to 86.7
50.0 to 69.9
25.0 to 49.9
12.9 to 24.9
5.0 to 12.8
1.0 to 4.9
0.0 to 0.9

U.S. percent is 12.9

Data Source: U.S. Census Bureau, Census 2000 Redistricting Data (PL 94-171) Summary File. Cartography: Population Division, U.S. Census Bureau. American FactFinder at *factfinder.census.gov* provides census data and mapping tools.

0   100 Miles

0   100 Miles

0   100 Miles

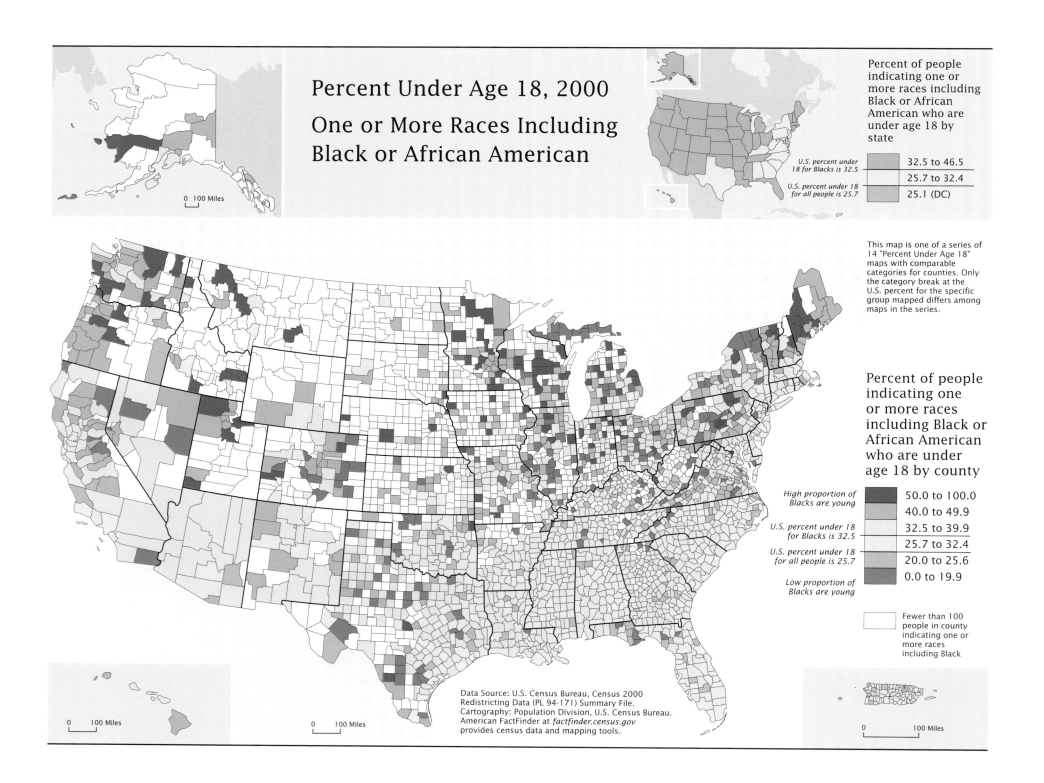

Percent Under Age 18, 2000
One or More Races Including Black or African American

0 100 Miles

Percent of people indicating one or more races including Black or African American who are under age 18 by state

U.S. percent under 18 for Blacks is 32.5

U.S. percent under 18 for all people is 25.7

	32.5 to 46.5
	25.7 to 32.4
	25.1 (DC)

This map is one of a series of 14 "Percent Under Age 18" maps with comparable categories for counties. Only the category break at the U.S. percent for the specific group mapped differs among maps in the series.

Percent of people indicating one or more races including Black or African American who are under age 18 by county

High proportion of Blacks are young

U.S. percent under 18 for Blacks is 32.5

U.S. percent under 18 for all people is 25.7

Low proportion of Blacks are young

	50.0 to 100.0
	40.0 to 49.9
	32.5 to 39.9
	25.7 to 32.4
	20.0 to 25.6
	0.0 to 19.9

Fewer than 100 people in county indicating one or more races including Black

Data Source: U.S. Census Bureau, Census 2000 Redistricting Data (PL 94-171) Summary File. Cartography: Population Division, U.S. Census Bureau. American FactFinder at *factfinder.census.gov* provides census data and mapping tools.

0 100 Miles

0 100 Miles

0 100 Miles

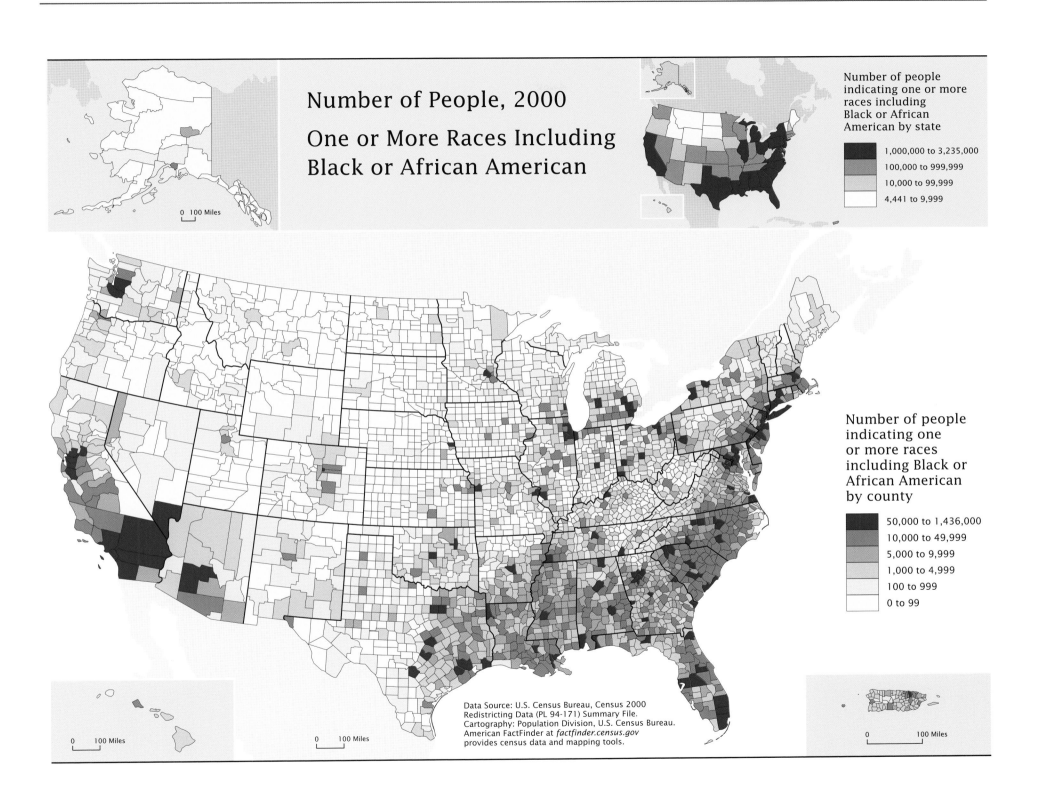

Number of People, 2000

One or More Races Including
Black or African American

Number of people
indicating one or more
races including
Black or African
American by state

1,000,000 to 3,235,000
100,000 to 999,999
10,000 to 99,999
4,441 to 9,999

Number of people
indicating one
or more races
including Black or
African American
by county

50,000 to 1,436,000
10,000 to 49,999
5,000 to 9,999
1,000 to 4,999
100 to 999
0 to 99

Data Source: U.S. Census Bureau, Census 2000
Redistricting Data (PL 94-171) Summary File.
Cartography: Population Division, U.S. Census Bureau.
American FactFinder at *factfinder.census.gov*
provides census data and mapping tools.

0 100 Miles

0 100 Miles

0 100 Miles

0 100 Miles

American Indian and Alaska Native

One race: **American Indian and Alaska Native**

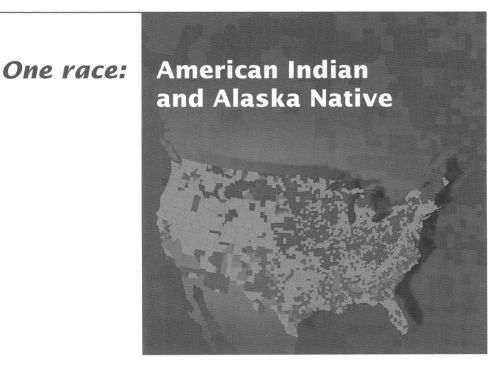

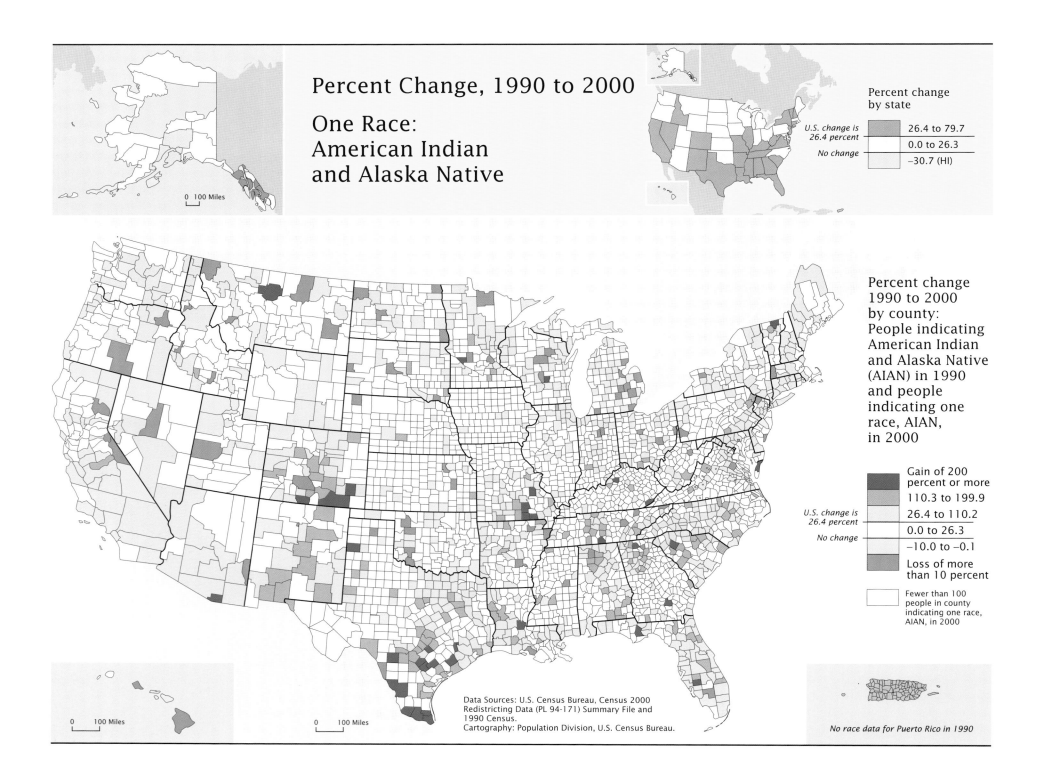

Percent Change, 1990 to 2000

One Race:
American Indian
and Alaska Native

Percent change
by state

U.S. change is
26.4 percent

No change

26.4 to 79.7

0.0 to 26.3

−30.7 (HI)

Percent change
1990 to 2000
by county:
People indicating
American Indian
and Alaska Native
(AIAN) in 1990
and people
indicating one
race, AIAN,
in 2000

Gain of 200
percent or more

110.3 to 199.9

U.S. change is
26.4 percent

26.4 to 110.2

0.0 to 26.3

No change

−10.0 to −0.1

Loss of more
than 10 percent

Fewer than 100
people in county
indicating one race,
AIAN, in 2000

0   100 Miles

0   100 Miles

0   100 Miles

Data Sources: U.S. Census Bureau, Census 2000
Redistricting Data (PL 94-171) Summary File and
1990 Census.
Cartography: Population Division, U.S. Census Bureau.

No race data for Puerto Rico in 1990

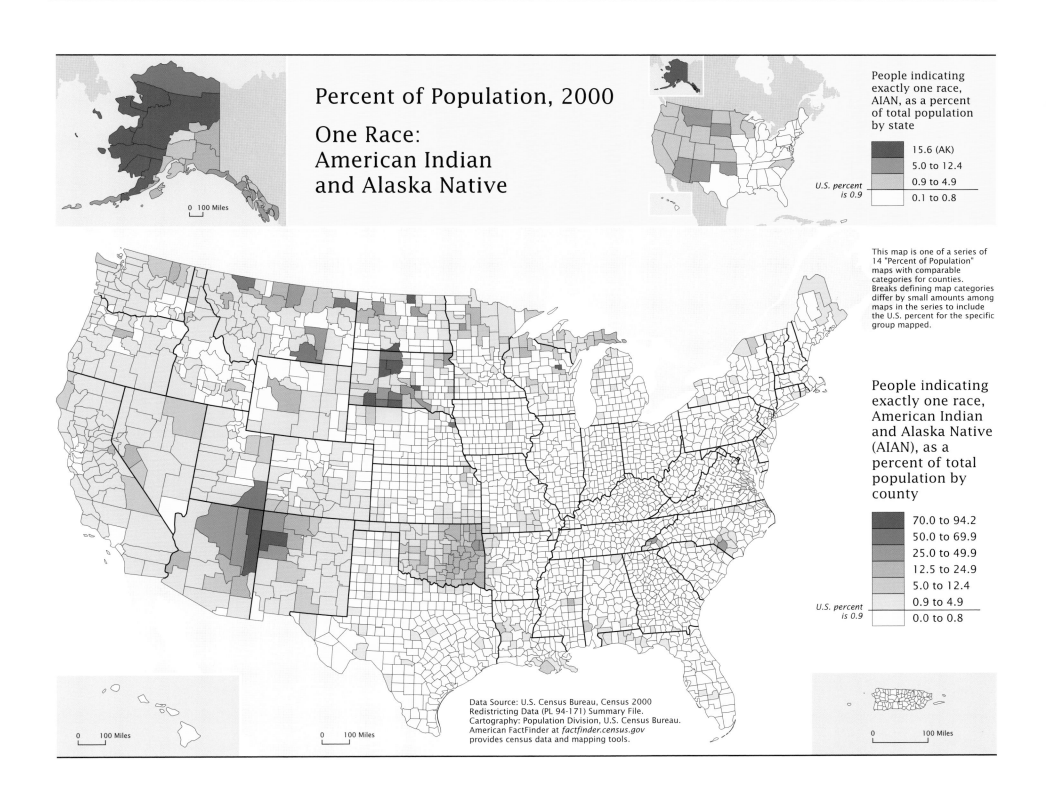

Percent of Population, 2000

One Race:
American Indian
and Alaska Native

People indicating
exactly one race,
AIAN, as a percent
of total population
by state

	15.6 (AK)
	5.0 to 12.4
	0.9 to 4.9
	0.1 to 0.8

*U.S. percent
is 0.9*

This map is one of a series of
14 "Percent of Population"
maps with comparable
categories for counties.
Breaks defining map categories
differ by small amounts among
maps in the series to include
the U.S. percent for the specific
group mapped.

People indicating
exactly one race,
American Indian
and Alaska Native
(AIAN), as a
percent of total
population by
county

	70.0 to 94.2
	50.0 to 69.9
	25.0 to 49.9
	12.5 to 24.9
	5.0 to 12.4
	0.9 to 4.9
	0.0 to 0.8

*U.S. percent
is 0.9*

Data Source: U.S. Census Bureau, Census 2000
Redistricting Data (PL 94-171) Summary File.
Cartography: Population Division, U.S. Census Bureau.
American FactFinder at *factfinder.census.gov*
provides census data and mapping tools.

0 100 Miles

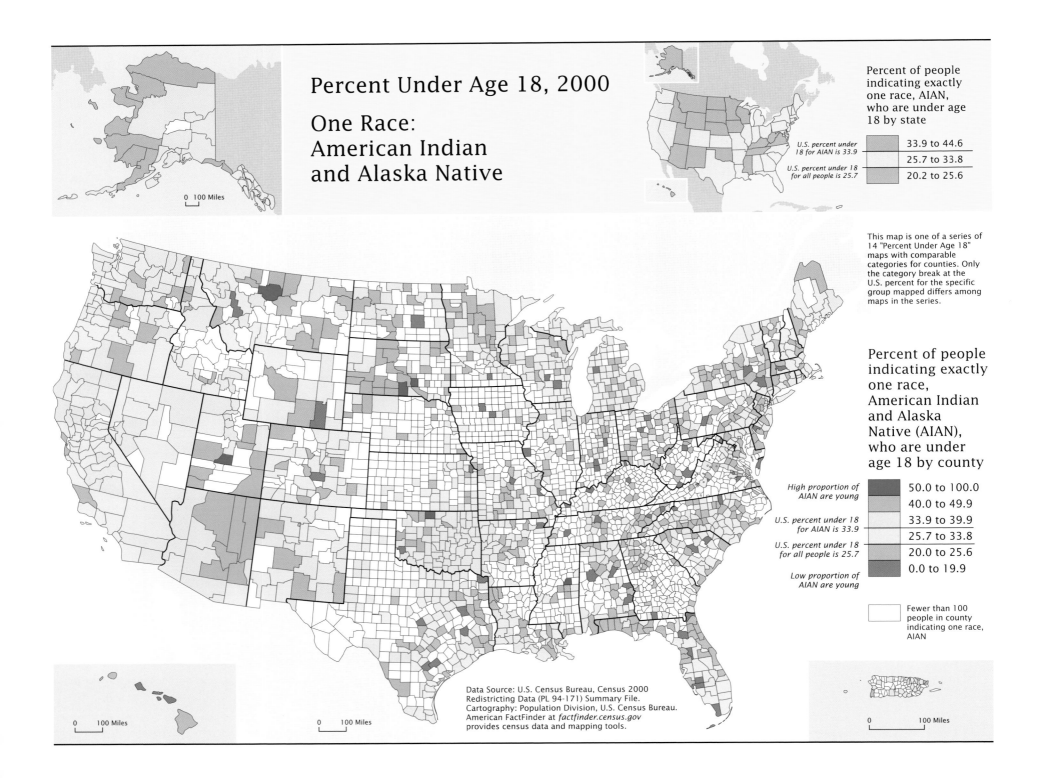

Percent Under Age 18, 2000

One Race:
American Indian
and Alaska Native

Percent of people indicating exactly one race, AIAN, who are under age 18 by state

U.S. percent under 18 for AIAN is 33.9

U.S. percent under 18 for all people is 25.7

	33.9 to 44.6
	25.7 to 33.8
	20.2 to 25.6

This map is one of a series of 14 "Percent Under Age 18" maps with comparable categories for counties. Only the category break at the U.S. percent for the specific group mapped differs among maps in the series.

Percent of people indicating exactly one race, American Indian and Alaska Native (AIAN), who are under age 18 by county

High proportion of AIAN are young

U.S. percent under 18 for AIAN is 33.9

U.S. percent under 18 for all people is 25.7

Low proportion of AIAN are young

	50.0 to 100.0
	40.0 to 49.9
	33.9 to 39.9
	25.7 to 33.8
	20.0 to 25.6
	0.0 to 19.9

Fewer than 100 people in county indicating one race, AIAN

Data Source: U.S. Census Bureau, Census 2000 Redistricting Data (PL 94-171) Summary File.
Cartography: Population Division, U.S. Census Bureau.
American FactFinder at *factfinder.census.gov* provides census data and mapping tools.

0 100 Miles

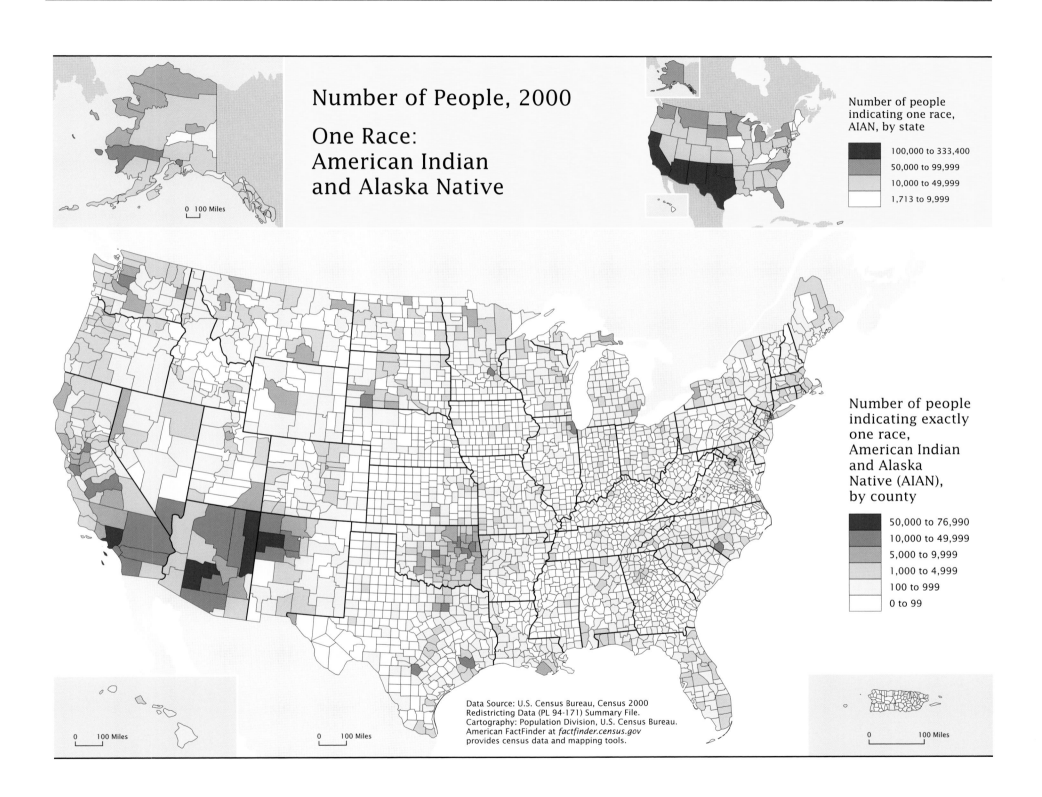

Number of People, 2000

One Race:
American Indian
and Alaska Native

0 100 Miles

Number of people
indicating one race,
AIAN, by state

- 100,000 to 333,400
- 50,000 to 99,999
- 10,000 to 49,999
- 1,713 to 9,999

Number of people
indicating exactly
one race,
American Indian
and Alaska
Native (AIAN),
by county

- 50,000 to 76,990
- 10,000 to 49,999
- 5,000 to 9,999
- 1,000 to 4,999
- 100 to 999
- 0 to 99

Data Source: U.S. Census Bureau, Census 2000
Redistricting Data (PL 94-171) Summary File.
Cartography: Population Division, U.S. Census Bureau.
American FactFinder at *factfinder.census.gov*
provides census data and mapping tools.

0 100 Miles

0 100 Miles

0   100 Miles

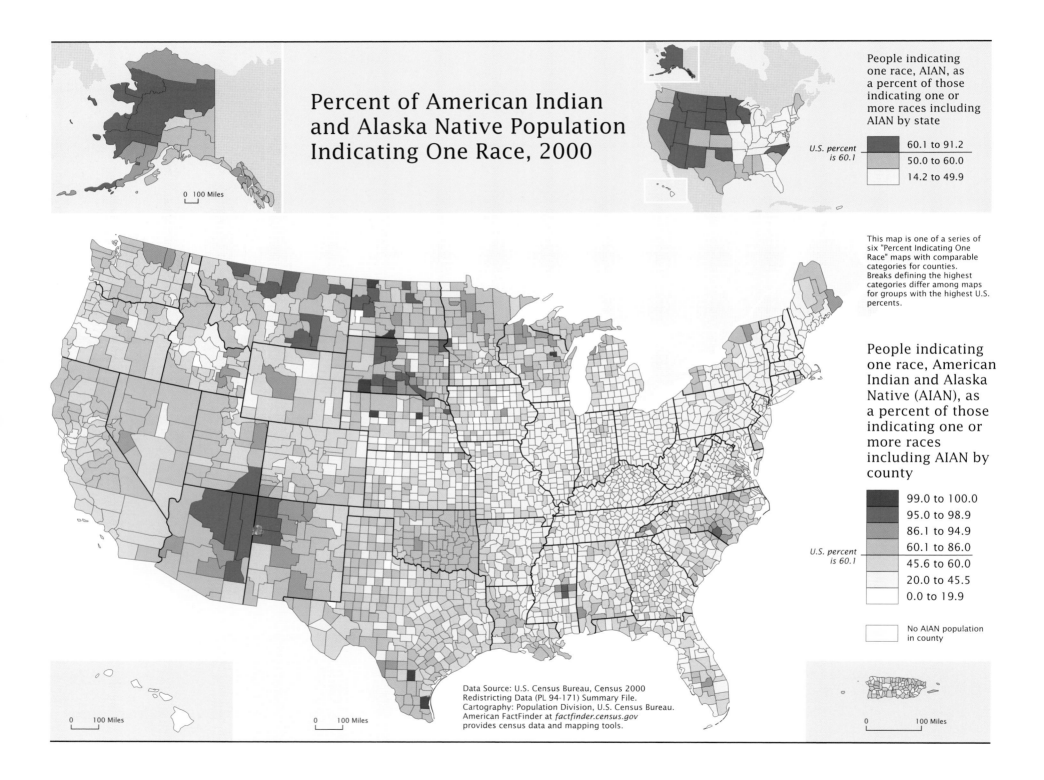

Percent of American Indian and Alaska Native Population Indicating One Race, 2000

People indicating one race, AIAN, as a percent of those indicating one or more races including AIAN by state

U.S. percent is 60.1

■	60.1 to 91.2
▨	50.0 to 60.0
□	14.2 to 49.9

This map is one of a series of six "Percent Indicating One Race" maps with comparable categories for counties. Breaks defining the highest categories differ among maps for groups with the highest U.S. percents.

People indicating one race, American Indian and Alaska Native (AIAN), as a percent of those indicating one or more races including AIAN by county

■	99.0 to 100.0
■	95.0 to 98.9
▨	86.1 to 94.9
▨	60.1 to 86.0
U.S. percent is 60.1 —	45.6 to 60.0
□	20.0 to 45.5
□	0.0 to 19.9

□	No AIAN population in county

0   100 Miles

Data Source: U.S. Census Bureau, Census 2000 Redistricting Data (PL 94-171) Summary File.
Cartography: Population Division, U.S. Census Bureau.
American FactFinder at *factfinder.census.gov* provides census data and mapping tools.

0   100 Miles

0   100 Miles

0   100 Miles

American Indian and Alaska Native

One or more races including **American Indian and Alaska Native**

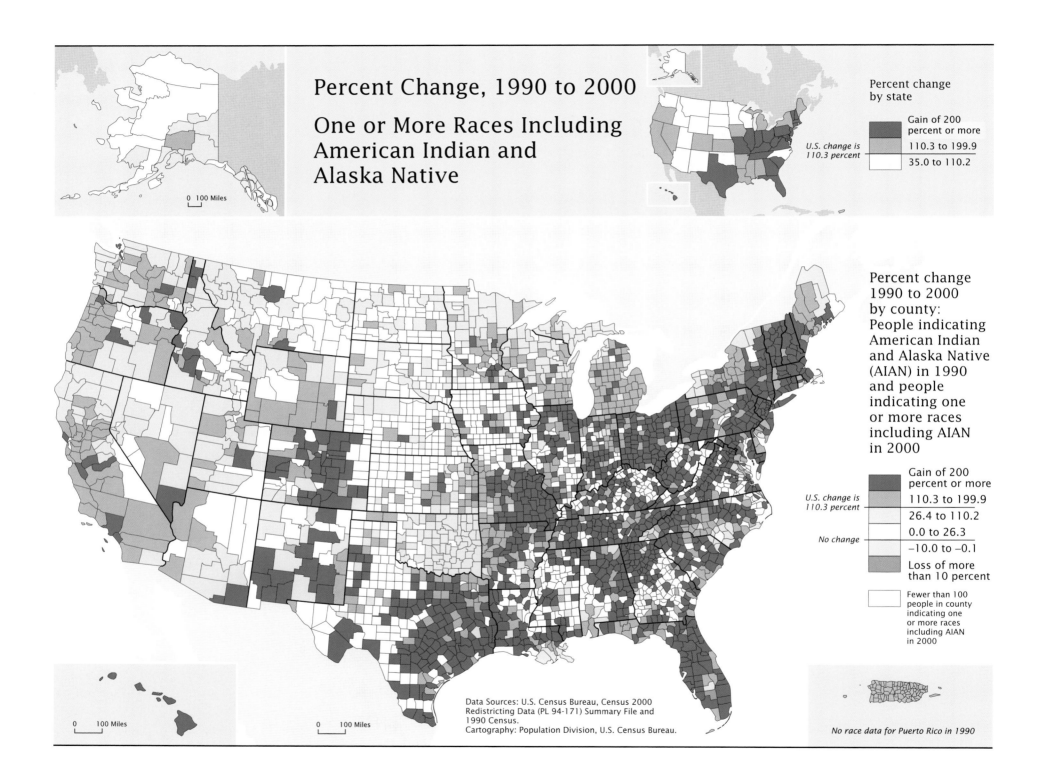

Percent Change, 1990 to 2000

One or More Races Including American Indian and Alaska Native

0 100 Miles

Percent change by state

U.S. change is 110.3 percent

Gain of 200 percent or more
110.3 to 199.9
35.0 to 110.2

Percent change 1990 to 2000 by county: People indicating American Indian and Alaska Native (AIAN) in 1990 and people indicating one or more races including AIAN in 2000

U.S. change is 110.3 percent

No change

Gain of 200 percent or more
110.3 to 199.9
26.4 to 110.2
0.0 to 26.3
−10.0 to −0.1
Loss of more than 10 percent

Fewer than 100 people in county indicating one or more races including AIAN in 2000

0 100 Miles

0 100 Miles

Data Sources: U.S. Census Bureau, Census 2000 Redistricting Data (PL 94-171) Summary File and 1990 Census.
Cartography: Population Division, U.S. Census Bureau.

No race data for Puerto Rico in 1990

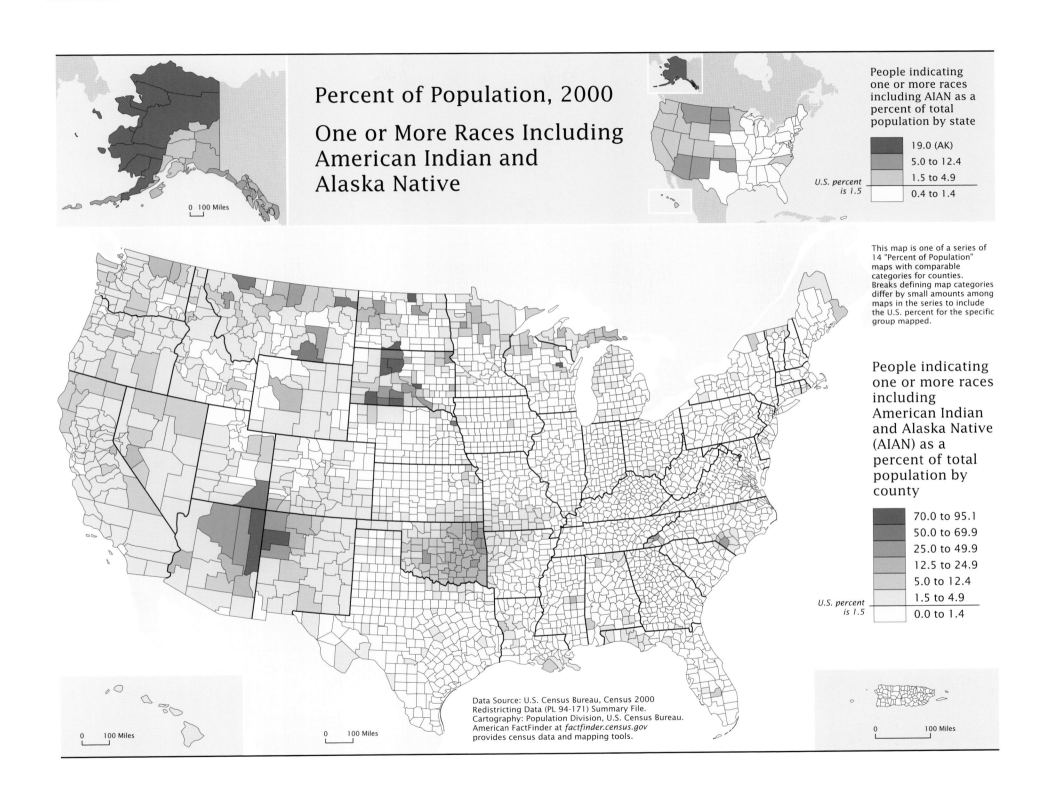

Percent of Population, 2000

One or More Races Including
American Indian and
Alaska Native

0 100 Miles

People indicating
one or more races
including AIAN as a
percent of total
population by state

19.0 (AK)
5.0 to 12.4
1.5 to 4.9

U.S. percent
is 1.5

0.4 to 1.4

This map is one of a series of
14 "Percent of Population"
maps with comparable
categories for counties.
Breaks defining map categories
differ by small amounts among
maps in the series to include
the U.S. percent for the specific
group mapped.

People indicating
one or more races
including
American Indian
and Alaska Native
(AIAN) as a
percent of total
population by
county

70.0 to 95.1
50.0 to 69.9
25.0 to 49.9
12.5 to 24.9
5.0 to 12.4
1.5 to 4.9

U.S. percent
is 1.5

0.0 to 1.4

Data Source: U.S. Census Bureau, Census 2000
Redistricting Data (PL 94-171) Summary File.
Cartography: Population Division, U.S. Census Bureau.
American FactFinder at *factfinder.census.gov*
provides census data and mapping tools.

0 100 Miles

0 100 Miles

0 100 Miles

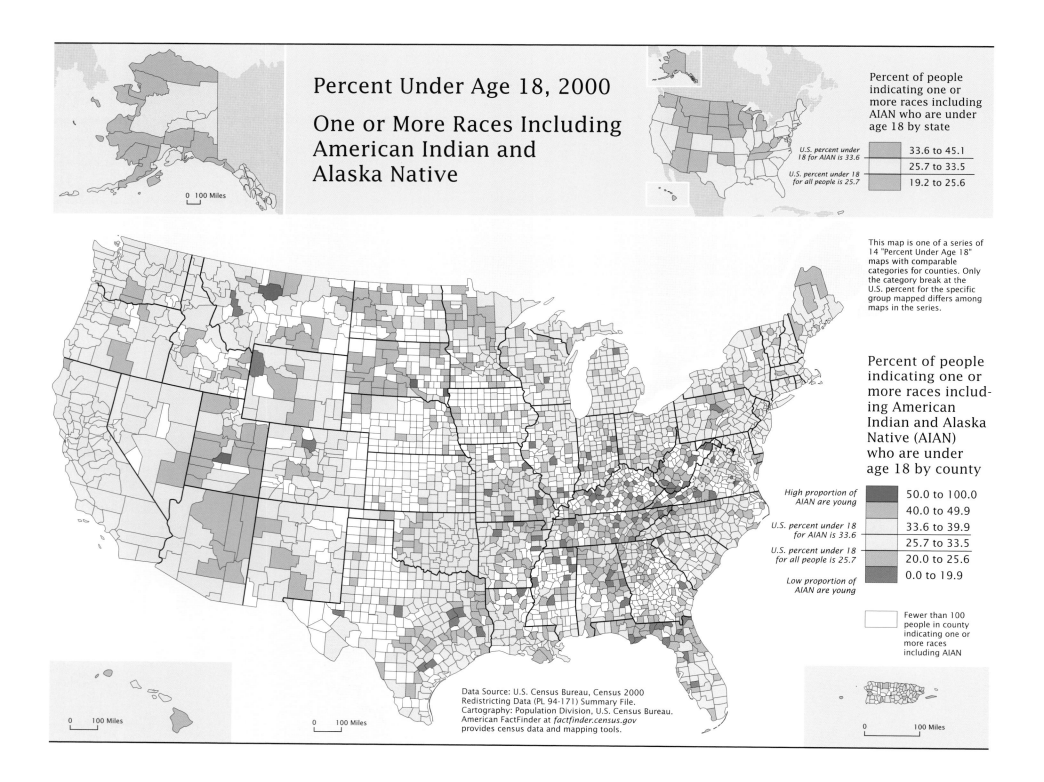

Percent Under Age 18, 2000

One or More Races Including American Indian and Alaska Native

0 100 Miles

Percent of people indicating one or more races including AIAN who are under age 18 by state

U.S. percent under 18 for AIAN is 33.6

U.S. percent under 18 for all people is 25.7

	33.6 to 45.1
	25.7 to 33.5
	19.2 to 25.6

This map is one of a series of 14 "Percent Under Age 18" maps with comparable categories for counties. Only the category break at the U.S. percent for the specific group mapped differs among maps in the series.

Percent of people indicating one or more races including American Indian and Alaska Native (AIAN) who are under age 18 by county

High proportion of AIAN are young

U.S. percent under 18 for AIAN is 33.6

U.S. percent under 18 for all people is 25.7

Low proportion of AIAN are young

	50.0 to 100.0
	40.0 to 49.9
	33.6 to 39.9
	25.7 to 33.5
	20.0 to 25.6
	0.0 to 19.9

Fewer than 100 people in county indicating one or more races including AIAN

0 100 Miles

0 100 Miles

Data Source: U.S. Census Bureau, Census 2000 Redistricting Data (PL 94-171) Summary File. Cartography: Population Division, U.S. Census Bureau. American FactFinder at *factfinder.census.gov* provides census data and mapping tools.

0 100 Miles

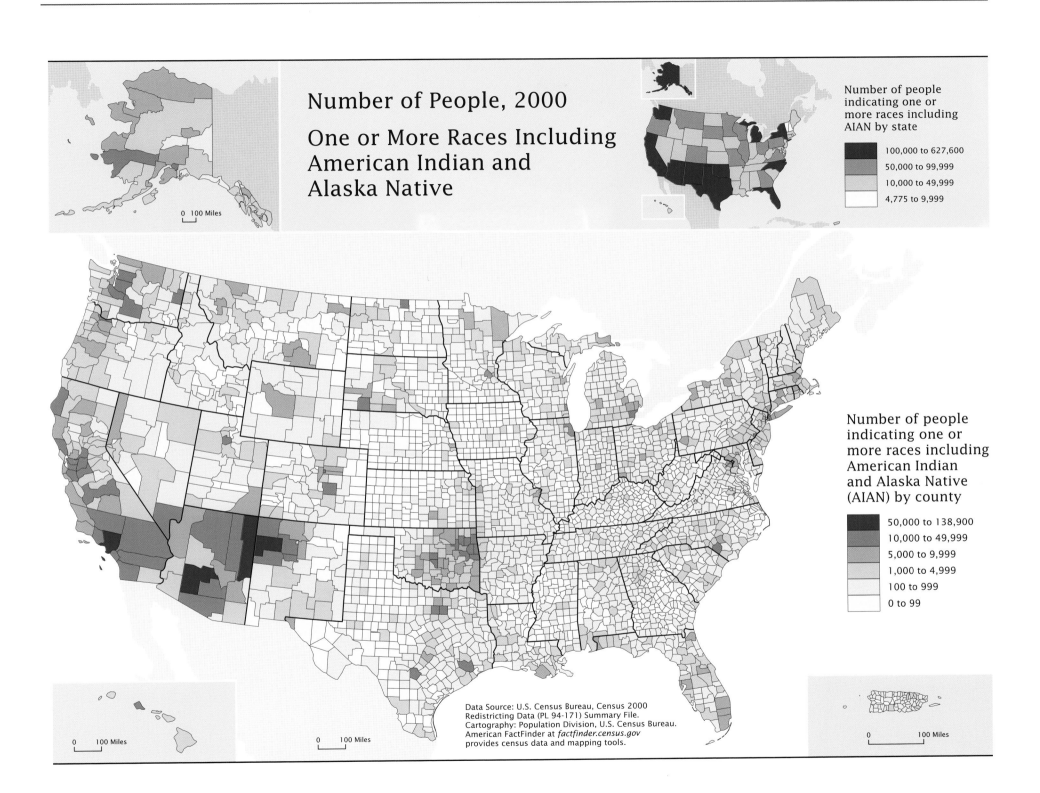

Number of People, 2000

One or More Races Including American Indian and Alaska Native

Number of people indicating one or more races including AIAN by state

100,000 to 627,600
50,000 to 99,999
10,000 to 49,999
4,775 to 9,999

Number of people indicating one or more races including American Indian and Alaska Native (AIAN) by county

50,000 to 138,900
10,000 to 49,999
5,000 to 9,999
1,000 to 4,999
100 to 999
0 to 99

0 100 Miles

Data Source: U.S. Census Bureau, Census 2000 Redistricting Data (PL 94-171) Summary File. Cartography: Population Division, U.S. Census Bureau. American FactFinder at *factfinder.census.gov* provides census data and mapping tools.

0 100 Miles

0 100 Miles

Asian

One race: Asian

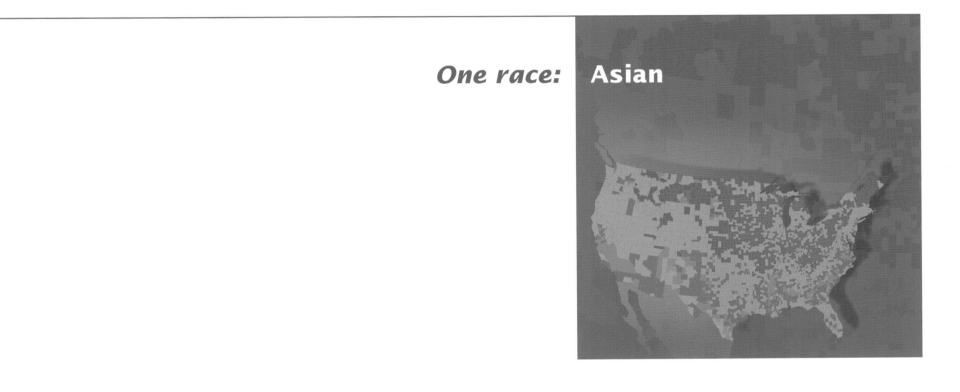

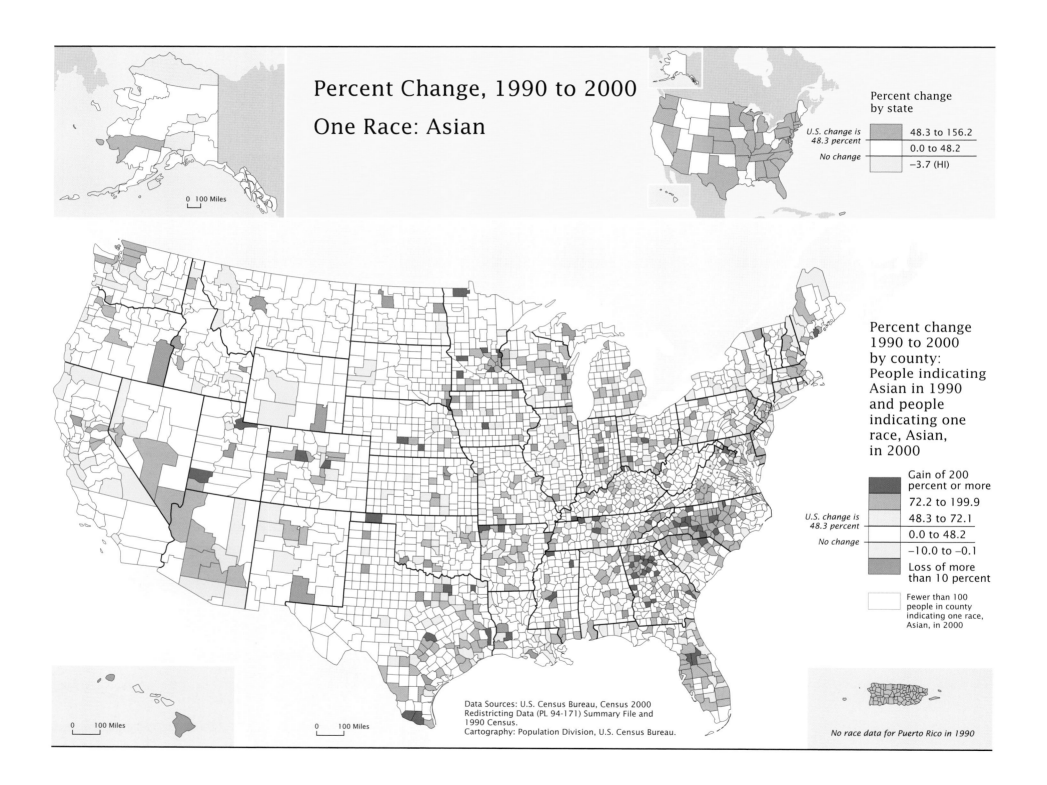

Percent Change, 1990 to 2000

One Race: Asian

Percent change
by state

U.S. change is
48.3 percent — 48.3 to 156.2

0.0 to 48.2

No change — −3.7 (HI)

Percent change
1990 to 2000
by county:
People indicating
Asian in 1990
and people
indicating one
race, Asian,
in 2000

Gain of 200
percent or more

72.2 to 199.9

U.S. change is
48.3 percent — 48.3 to 72.1

0.0 to 48.2

No change — −10.0 to −0.1

Loss of more
than 10 percent

Fewer than 100
people in county
indicating one race,
Asian, in 2000

Data Sources: U.S. Census Bureau, Census 2000
Redistricting Data (PL 94-171) Summary File and
1990 Census.
Cartography: Population Division, U.S. Census Bureau.

0   100 Miles

0   100 Miles

No race data for Puerto Rico in 1990

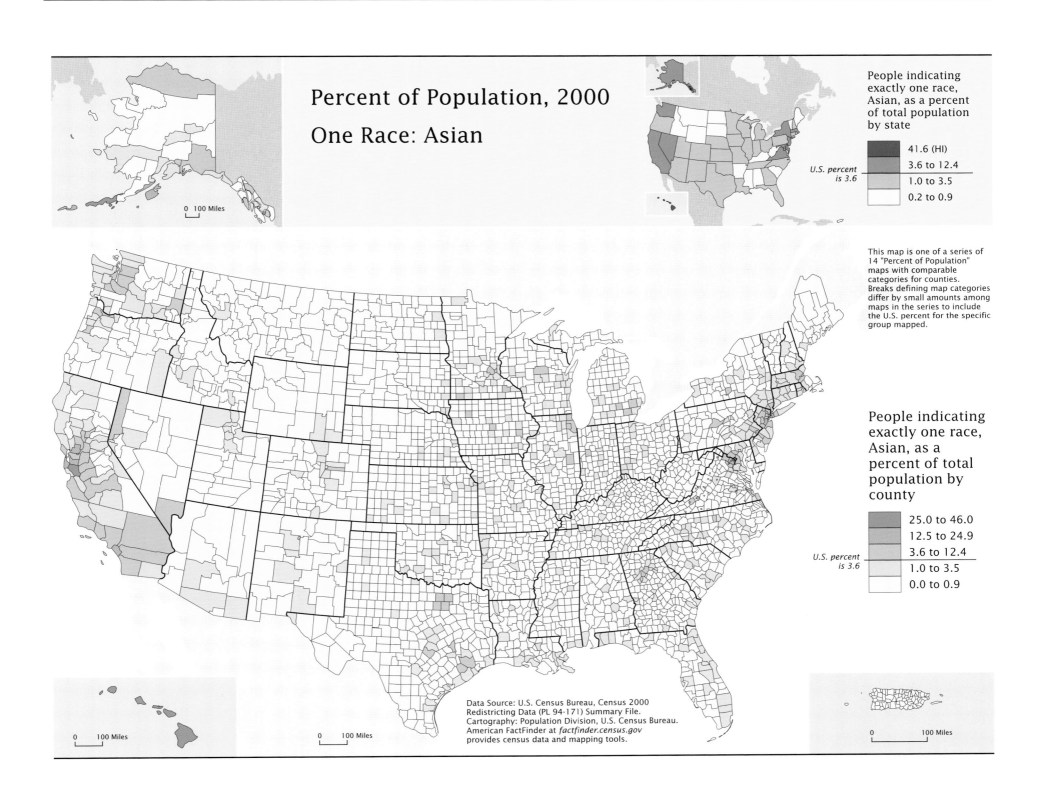

Percent of Population, 2000

One Race: Asian

People indicating exactly one race, Asian, as a percent of total population by state

U.S. percent is 3.6

41.6 (HI)
3.6 to 12.4
1.0 to 3.5
0.2 to 0.9

This map is one of a series of 14 "Percent of Population" maps with comparable categories for counties. Breaks defining map categories differ by small amounts among maps in the series to include the U.S. percent for the specific group mapped.

People indicating exactly one race, Asian, as a percent of total population by county

U.S. percent is 3.6

25.0 to 46.0
12.5 to 24.9
3.6 to 12.4
1.0 to 3.5
0.0 to 0.9

0 100 Miles

0 100 Miles

0 100 Miles

0 100 Miles

Data Source: U.S. Census Bureau, Census 2000 Redistricting Data (PL 94-171) Summary File. Cartography: Population Division, U.S. Census Bureau. American FactFinder at *factfinder.census.gov* provides census data and mapping tools.

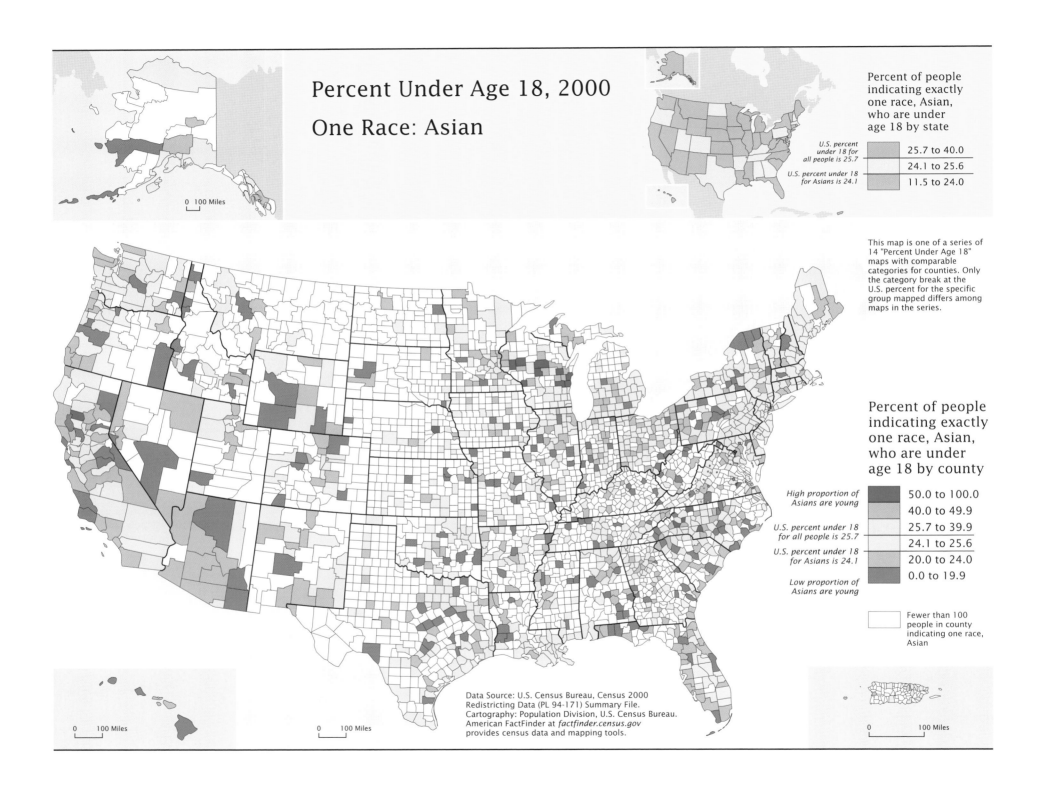

Percent Under Age 18, 2000

One Race: Asian

Percent of people indicating exactly one race, Asian, who are under age 18 by state

U.S. percent under 18 for all people is 25.7
U.S. percent under 18 for Asians is 24.1

	25.7 to 40.0
	24.1 to 25.6
	11.5 to 24.0

This map is one of a series of 14 "Percent Under Age 18" maps with comparable categories for counties. Only the category break at the U.S. percent for the specific group mapped differs among maps in the series.

Percent of people indicating exactly one race, Asian, who are under age 18 by county

High proportion of Asians are young

U.S. percent under 18 for all people is 25.7

U.S. percent under 18 for Asians is 24.1

Low proportion of Asians are young

	50.0 to 100.0
	40.0 to 49.9
	25.7 to 39.9
	24.1 to 25.6
	20.0 to 24.0
	0.0 to 19.9

Fewer than 100 people in county indicating one race, Asian

Data Source: U.S. Census Bureau, Census 2000 Redistricting Data (PL 94-171) Summary File. Cartography: Population Division, U.S. Census Bureau. American FactFinder at *factfinder.census.gov* provides census data and mapping tools.

0 100 Miles

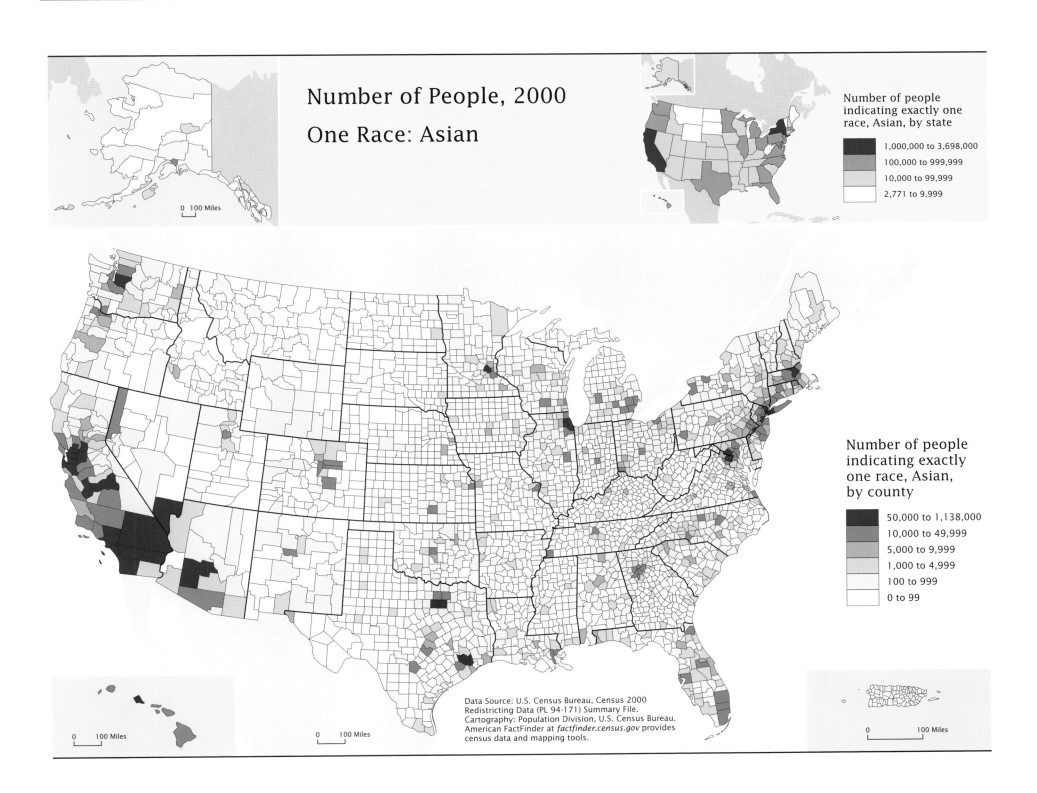

Number of People, 2000

One Race: Asian

Number of people
indicating exactly one
race, Asian, by state

■ 1,000,000 to 3,698,000
■ 100,000 to 999,999
■ 10,000 to 99,999
□ 2,771 to 9,999

Number of people
indicating exactly
one race, Asian,
by county

■ 50,000 to 1,138,000
■ 10,000 to 49,999
■ 5,000 to 9,999
■ 1,000 to 4,999
□ 100 to 999
□ 0 to 99

0 100 Miles

0 100 Miles

0 100 Miles

0 100 Miles

Data Source: U.S. Census Bureau, Census 2000
Redistricting Data (PL 94-171) Summary File.
Cartography: Population Division, U.S. Census Bureau.
American FactFinder at *factfinder.census.gov* provides
census data and mapping tools.

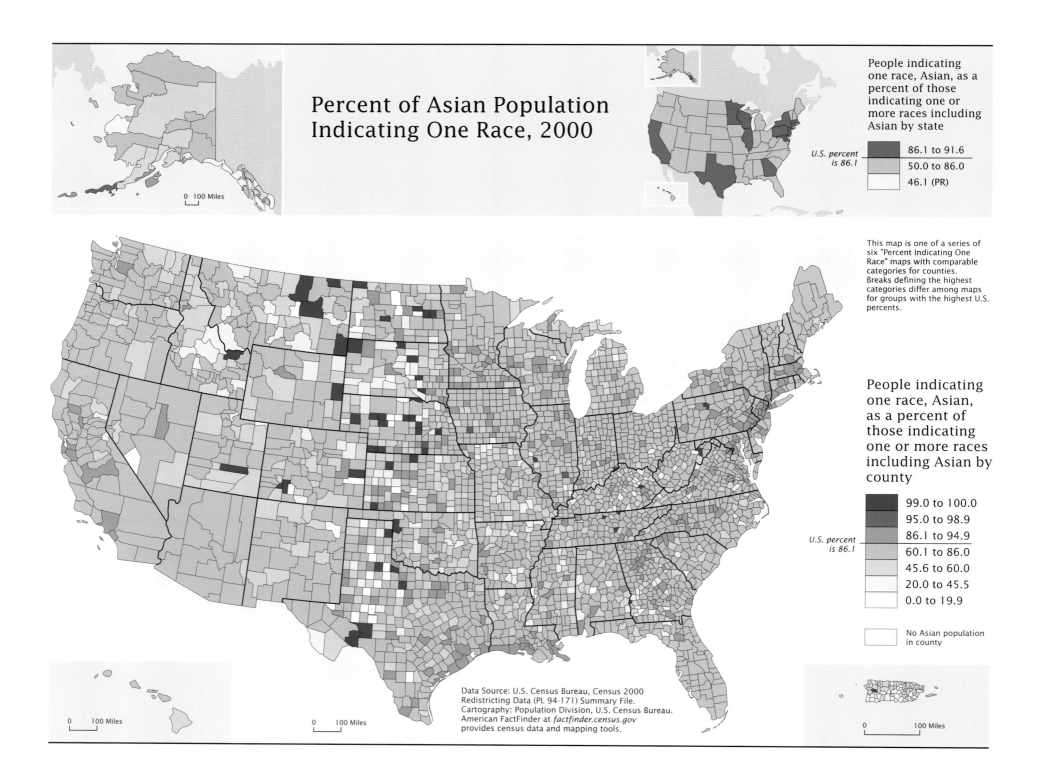

Percent of Asian Population Indicating One Race, 2000

People indicating one race, Asian, as a percent of those indicating one or more races including Asian by state

U.S. percent is 86.1

- 86.1 to 91.6
- 50.0 to 86.0
- 46.1 (PR)

This map is one of a series of six "Percent Indicating One Race" maps with comparable categories for counties. Breaks defining the highest categories differ among maps for groups with the highest U.S. percents.

People indicating one race, Asian, as a percent of those indicating one or more races including Asian by county

U.S. percent is 86.1

- 99.0 to 100.0
- 95.0 to 98.9
- 86.1 to 94.9
- 60.1 to 86.0
- 45.6 to 60.0
- 20.0 to 45.5
- 0.0 to 19.9

- No Asian population in county

0 100 Miles

Data Source: U.S. Census Bureau, Census 2000 Redistricting Data (PL 94-171) Summary File. Cartography: Population Division, U.S. Census Bureau. American FactFinder at *factfinder.census.gov* provides census data and mapping tools.

0 100 Miles

0 100 Miles

0 100 Miles

Asian

One or more races including **Asian**

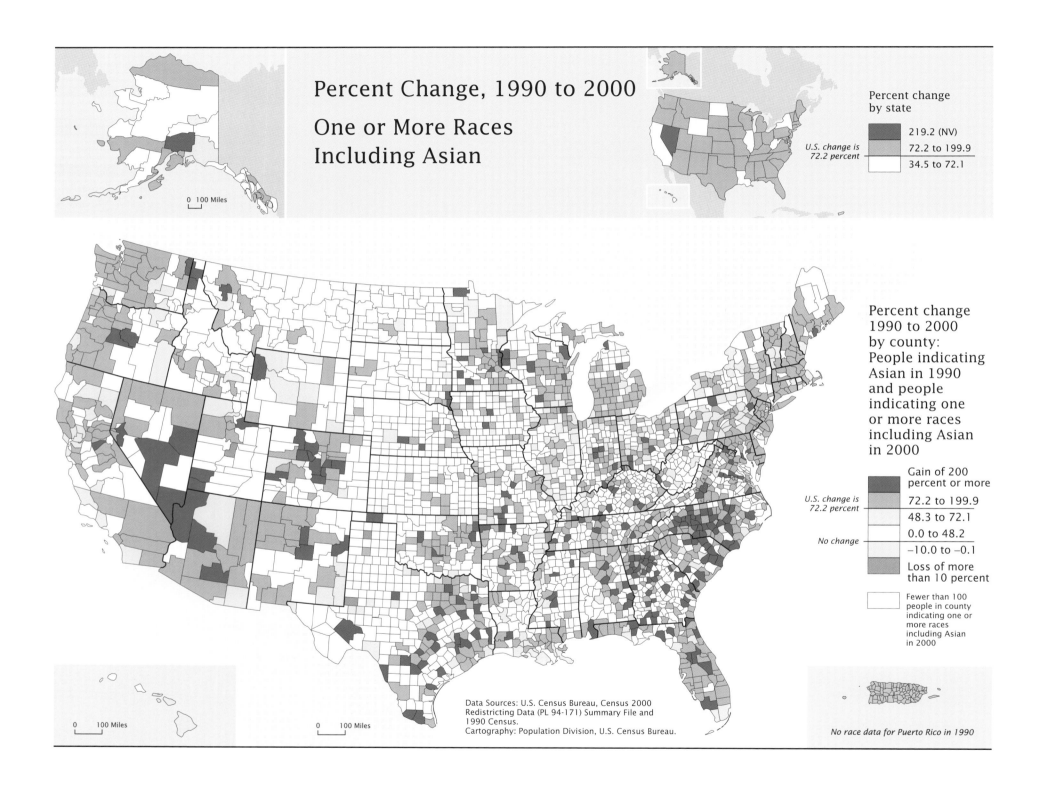

Percent Change, 1990 to 2000

One or More Races
Including Asian

Percent change
by state

*U.S. change is
72.2 percent*

■	219.2 (NV)
▨	72.2 to 199.9
□	34.5 to 72.1

Percent change
1990 to 2000
by county:
People indicating
Asian in 1990
and people
indicating one
or more races
including Asian
in 2000

*U.S. change is
72.2 percent*

No change

■	Gain of 200 percent or more
▨	72.2 to 199.9
	48.3 to 72.1
	0.0 to 48.2
	–10.0 to –0.1
▨	Loss of more than 10 percent
□	Fewer than 100 people in county indicating one or more races including Asian in 2000

0 100 Miles

Data Sources: U.S. Census Bureau, Census 2000
Redistricting Data (PL 94-171) Summary File and
1990 Census.
Cartography: Population Division, U.S. Census Bureau.

No race data for Puerto Rico in 1990

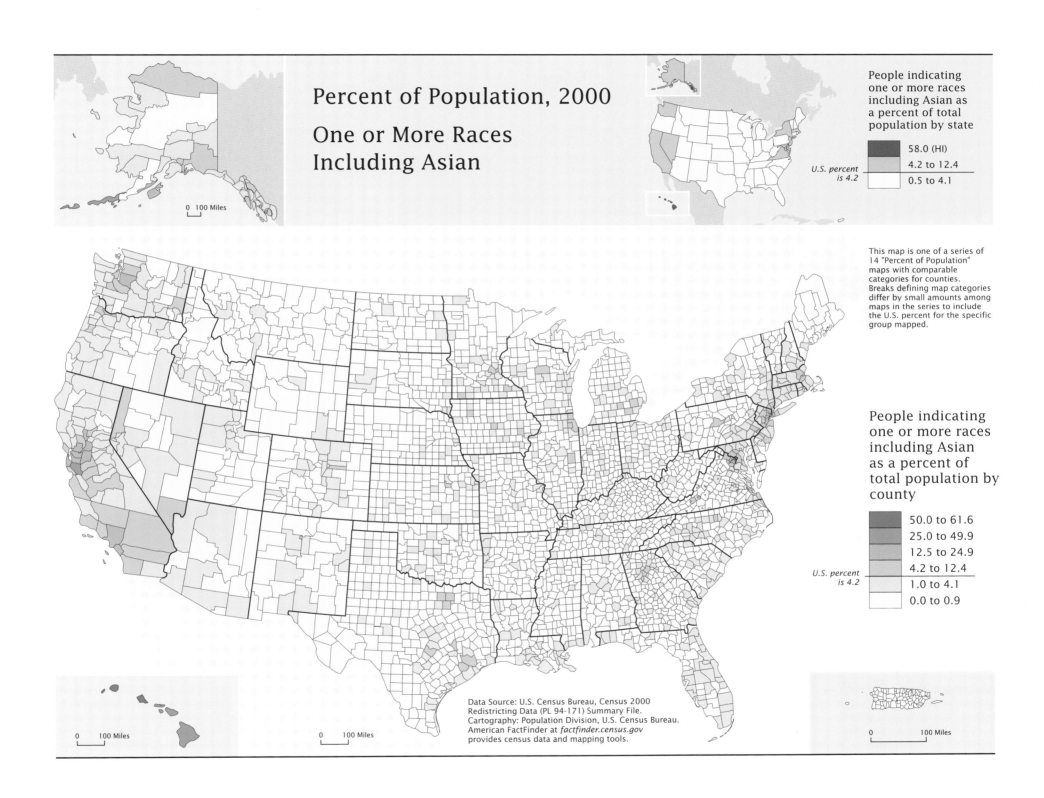

Percent of Population, 2000

One or More Races
Including Asian

People indicating
one or more races
including Asian as
a percent of total
population by state

	58.0 (HI)
U.S. percent is 4.2	4.2 to 12.4
	0.5 to 4.1

0 100 Miles

This map is one of a series of
14 "Percent of Population"
maps with comparable
categories for counties.
Breaks defining map categories
differ by small amounts among
maps in the series to include
the U.S. percent for the specific
group mapped.

People indicating
one or more races
including Asian
as a percent of
total population by
county

	50.0 to 61.6
	25.0 to 49.9
	12.5 to 24.9
U.S. percent is 4.2	4.2 to 12.4
	1.0 to 4.1
	0.0 to 0.9

0 100 Miles

Data Source: U.S. Census Bureau, Census 2000
Redistricting Data (PL 94-171) Summary File.
Cartography: Population Division, U.S. Census Bureau.
American FactFinder at *factfinder.census.gov*
provides census data and mapping tools.

0 100 Miles

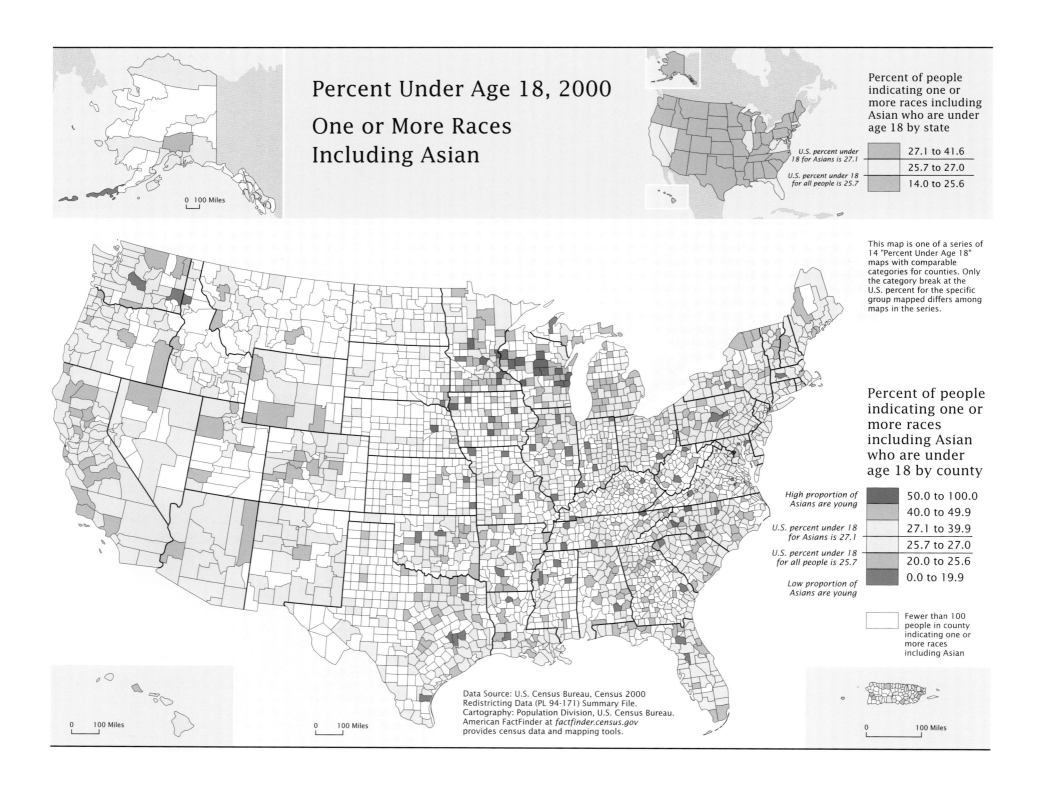

Percent Under Age 18, 2000

One or More Races
Including Asian

0 100 Miles

Percent of people
indicating one or
more races including
Asian who are under
age 18 by state

U.S. percent under
18 for Asians is 27.1

U.S. percent under 18
for all people is 25.7

	27.1 to 41.6
	25.7 to 27.0
	14.0 to 25.6

This map is one of a series of
14 "Percent Under Age 18"
maps with comparable
categories for counties. Only
the category break at the
U.S. percent for the specific
group mapped differs among
maps in the series.

Percent of people
indicating one or
more races
including Asian
who are under
age 18 by county

High proportion of
Asians are young

U.S. percent under 18
for Asians is 27.1

U.S. percent under 18
for all people is 25.7

Low proportion of
Asians are young

	50.0 to 100.0
	40.0 to 49.9
	27.1 to 39.9
	25.7 to 27.0
	20.0 to 25.6
	0.0 to 19.9

Fewer than 100
people in county
indicating one or
more races
including Asian

Data Source: U.S. Census Bureau, Census 2000
Redistricting Data (PL 94-171) Summary File.
Cartography: Population Division, U.S. Census Bureau.
American FactFinder at *factfinder.census.gov*
provides census data and mapping tools.

0 100 Miles

0 100 Miles

0 100 Miles

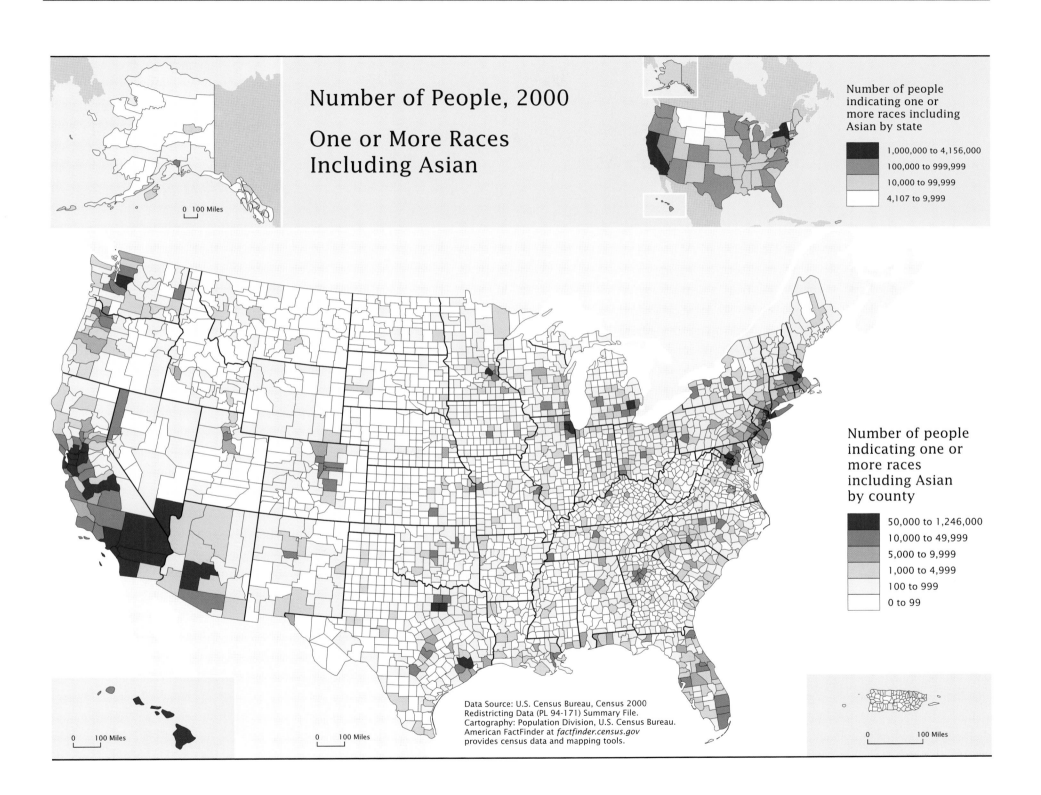

Number of People, 2000

One or More Races Including Asian

Number of people indicating one or more races including Asian by state

- 1,000,000 to 4,156,000
- 100,000 to 999,999
- 10,000 to 99,999
- 4,107 to 9,999

Number of people indicating one or more races including Asian by county

- 50,000 to 1,246,000
- 10,000 to 49,999
- 5,000 to 9,999
- 1,000 to 4,999
- 100 to 999
- 0 to 99

0 100 Miles

Data Source: U.S. Census Bureau, Census 2000 Redistricting Data (PL 94-171) Summary File. Cartography: Population Division, U.S. Census Bureau. American FactFinder at *factfinder.census.gov* provides census data and mapping tools.

0 100 Miles

0 100 Miles

0 100 Miles

Native Hawaiian and Other Pacific Islander

One race:  **Native Hawaiian and Other Pacific Islander**

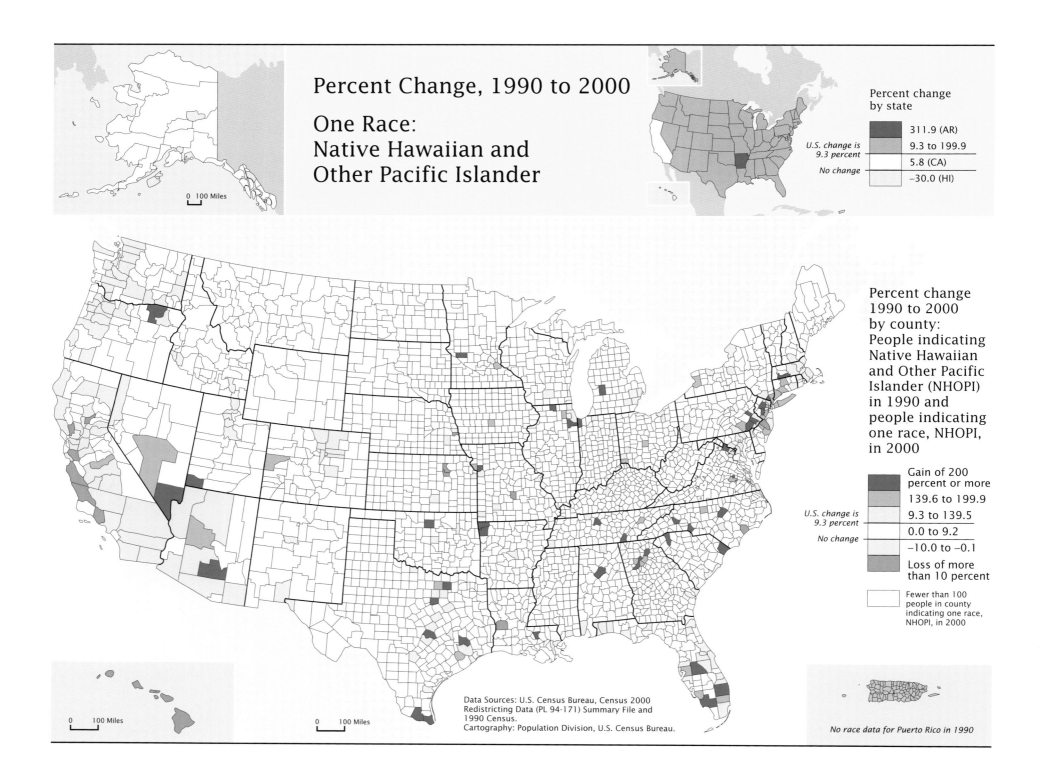

Percent Change, 1990 to 2000

One Race:
Native Hawaiian and
Other Pacific Islander

Percent change
by state

U.S. change is
9.3 percent

No change

311.9 (AR)
9.3 to 199.9
5.8 (CA)
−30.0 (HI)

Percent change
1990 to 2000
by county:
People indicating
Native Hawaiian
and Other Pacific
Islander (NHOPI)
in 1990 and
people indicating
one race, NHOPI,
in 2000

U.S. change is
9.3 percent

No change

Gain of 200
percent or more
139.6 to 199.9
9.3 to 139.5
0.0 to 9.2
−10.0 to −0.1
Loss of more
than 10 percent

Fewer than 100
people in county
indicating one race,
NHOPI, in 2000

Data Sources: U.S. Census Bureau, Census 2000
Redistricting Data (PL 94-171) Summary File and
1990 Census.
Cartography: Population Division, U.S. Census Bureau.

No race data for Puerto Rico in 1990

0   100 Miles

0   100 Miles

0   100 Miles

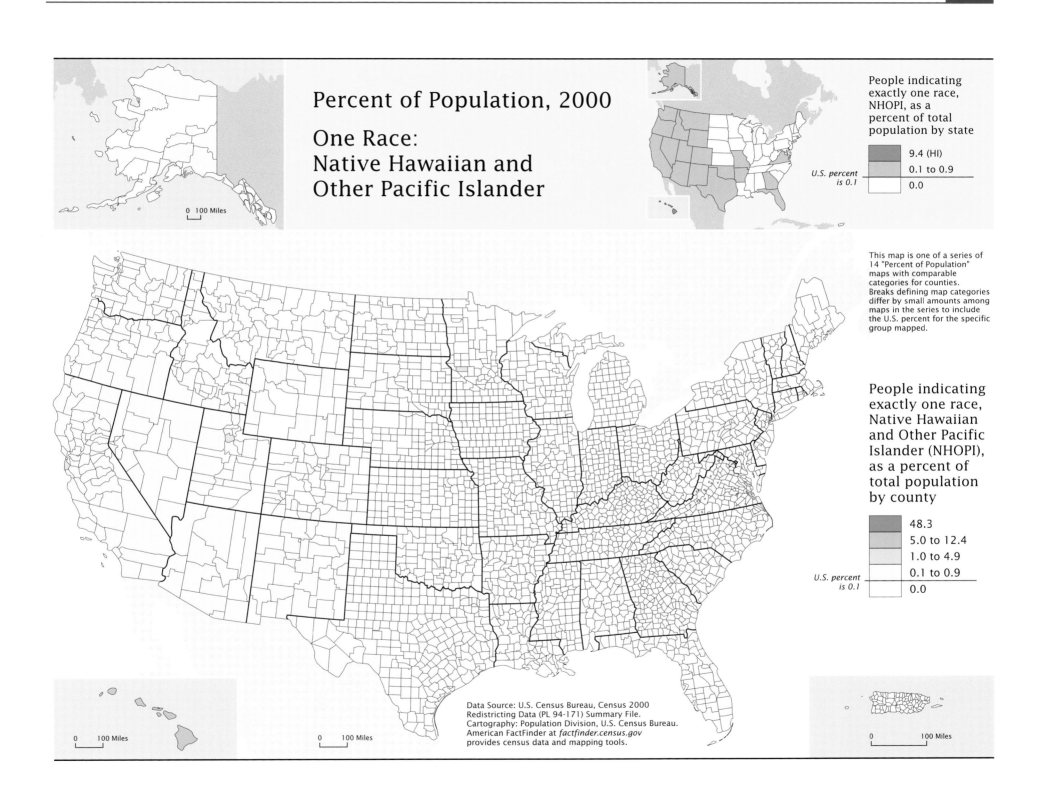

Percent of Population, 2000

One Race:
Native Hawaiian and
Other Pacific Islander

People indicating
exactly one race,
NHOPI, as a
percent of total
population by state

	9.4 (HI)
	0.1 to 0.9
U.S. percent is 0.1	0.0

This map is one of a series of 14 "Percent of Population" maps with comparable categories for counties. Breaks defining map categories differ by small amounts among maps in the series to include the U.S. percent for the specific group mapped.

People indicating
exactly one race,
Native Hawaiian
and Other Pacific
Islander (NHOPI),
as a percent of
total population
by county

	48.3
	5.0 to 12.4
	1.0 to 4.9
U.S. percent is 0.1	0.1 to 0.9
	0.0

0 100 Miles

0 100 Miles

0 100 Miles

Data Source: U.S. Census Bureau, Census 2000 Redistricting Data (PL 94-171) Summary File. Cartography: Population Division, U.S. Census Bureau. American FactFinder at *factfinder.census.gov* provides census data and mapping tools.

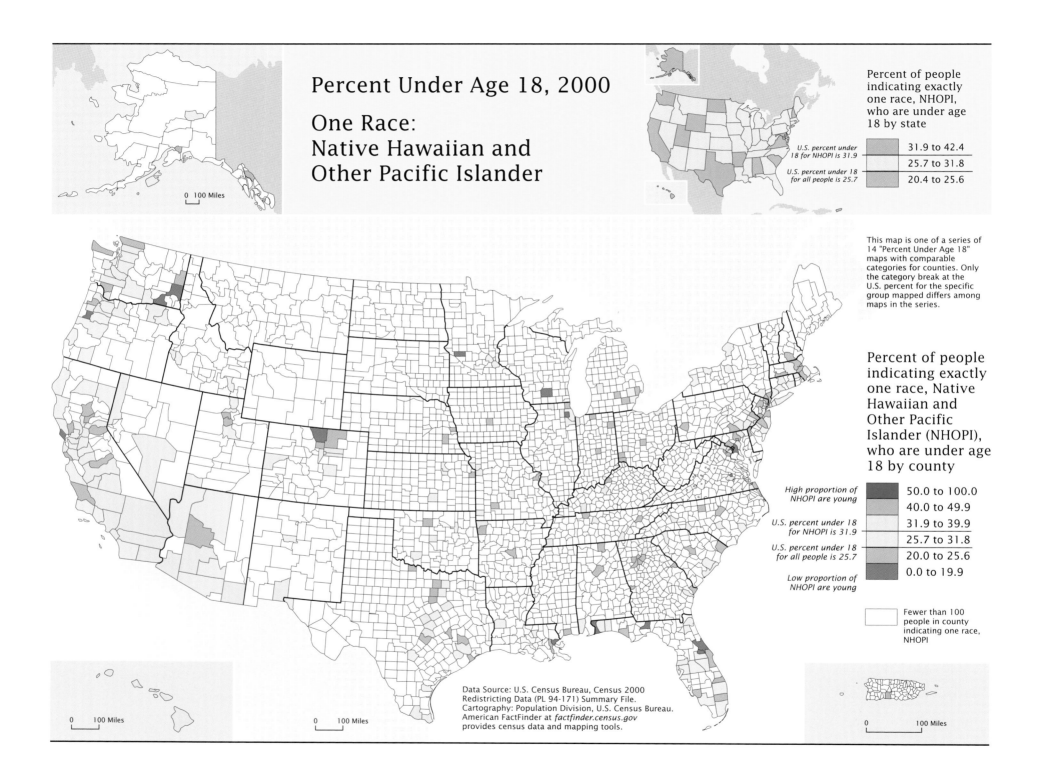

Percent Under Age 18, 2000

One Race:
Native Hawaiian and
Other Pacific Islander

0   100 Miles

Percent of people
indicating exactly
one race, NHOPI,
who are under age
18 by state

U.S. percent under
18 for NHOPI is 31.9

U.S. percent under 18
for all people is 25.7

	31.9 to 42.4
	25.7 to 31.8
	20.4 to 25.6

This map is one of a series of
14 "Percent Under Age 18"
maps with comparable
categories for counties. Only
the category break at the
U.S. percent for the specific
group mapped differs among
maps in the series.

Percent of people
indicating exactly
one race, Native
Hawaiian and
Other Pacific
Islander (NHOPI),
who are under age
18 by county

High proportion of
NHOPI are young

U.S. percent under 18
for NHOPI is 31.9

U.S. percent under 18
for all people is 25.7

Low proportion of
NHOPI are young

	50.0 to 100.0
	40.0 to 49.9
	31.9 to 39.9
	25.7 to 31.8
	20.0 to 25.6
	0.0 to 19.9

Fewer than 100
people in county
indicating one race,
NHOPI

0   100 Miles

0   100 Miles

Data Source: U.S. Census Bureau, Census 2000
Redistricting Data (PL 94-171) Summary File.
Cartography: Population Division, U.S. Census Bureau.
American FactFinder at factfinder.census.gov
provides census data and mapping tools.

0   100 Miles

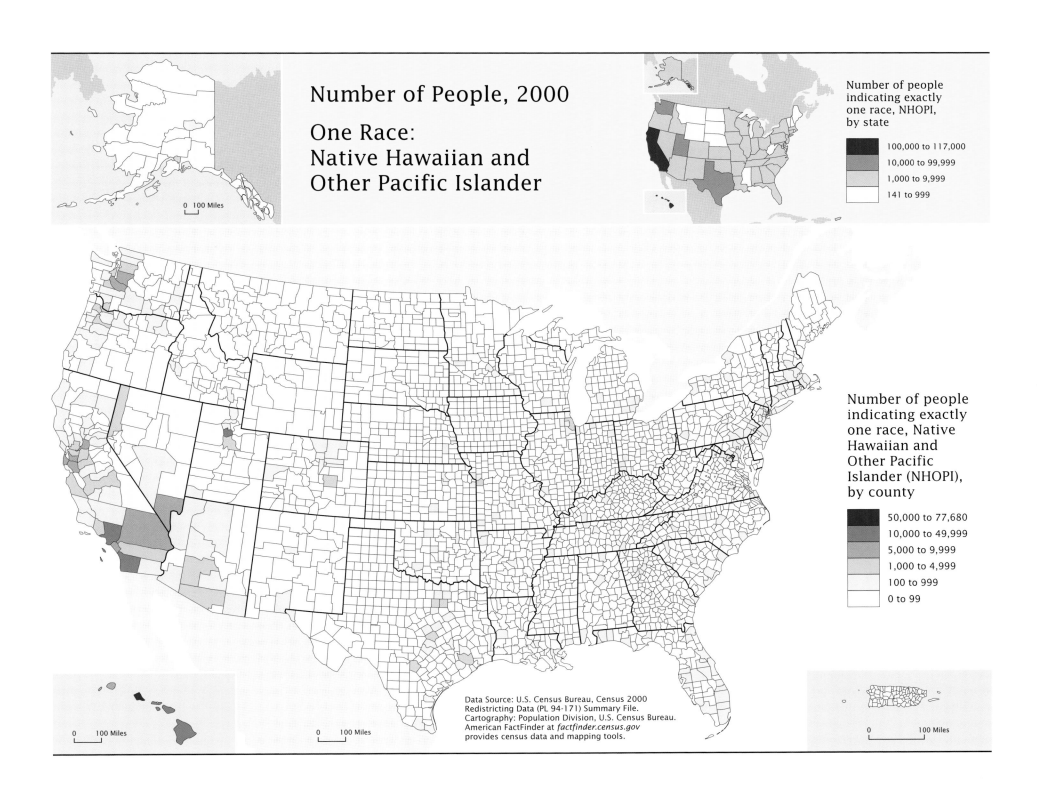

Number of People, 2000

One Race:
Native Hawaiian and
Other Pacific Islander

Number of people
indicating exactly
one race, NHOPI,
by state

- 100,000 to 117,000
- 10,000 to 99,999
- 1,000 to 9,999
- 141 to 999

Number of people
indicating exactly
one race, Native
Hawaiian and
Other Pacific
Islander (NHOPI),
by county

- 50,000 to 77,680
- 10,000 to 49,999
- 5,000 to 9,999
- 1,000 to 4,999
- 100 to 999
- 0 to 99

0   100 Miles

Data Source: U.S. Census Bureau, Census 2000
Redistricting Data (PL 94-171) Summary File.
Cartography: Population Division, U.S. Census Bureau.
American FactFinder at *factfinder.census.gov*
provides census data and mapping tools.

0   100 Miles

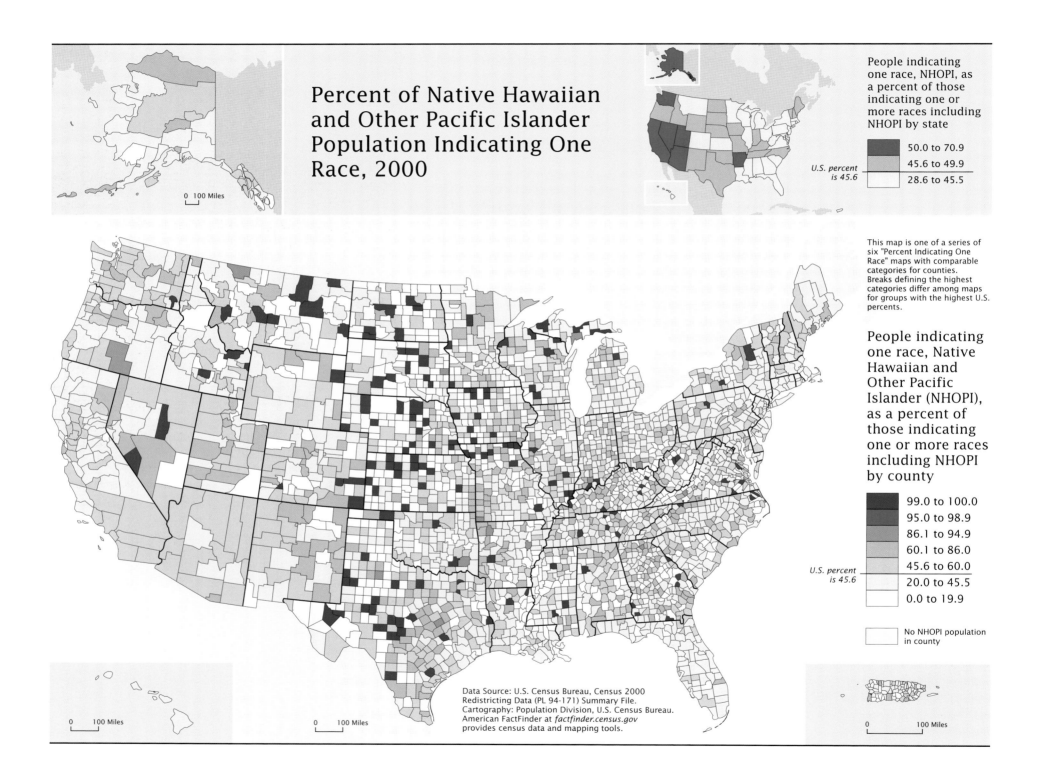

Percent of Native Hawaiian and Other Pacific Islander Population Indicating One Race, 2000

0 100 Miles

People indicating one race, NHOPI, as a percent of those indicating one or more races including NHOPI by state

▉	50.0 to 70.9
▩	45.6 to 49.9
☐	28.6 to 45.5

U.S. percent is 45.6

This map is one of a series of six "Percent Indicating One Race" maps with comparable categories for counties. Breaks defining the highest categories differ among maps for groups with the highest U.S. percents.

People indicating one race, Native Hawaiian and Other Pacific Islander (NHOPI), as a percent of those indicating one or more races including NHOPI by county

▉	99.0 to 100.0
▉	95.0 to 98.9
▩	86.1 to 94.9
▩	60.1 to 86.0
▨	45.6 to 60.0
☐	20.0 to 45.5
☐	0.0 to 19.9

U.S. percent is 45.6

☐	No NHOPI population in county

0 100 Miles

0 100 Miles

Data Source: U.S. Census Bureau, Census 2000 Redistricting Data (PL 94-171) Summary File. Cartography: Population Division, U.S. Census Bureau. American FactFinder at *factfinder.census.gov* provides census data and mapping tools.

0 100 Miles

Native Hawaiian and Other Pacific Islander

One or more races including Native Hawaiian and Other Pacific Islander

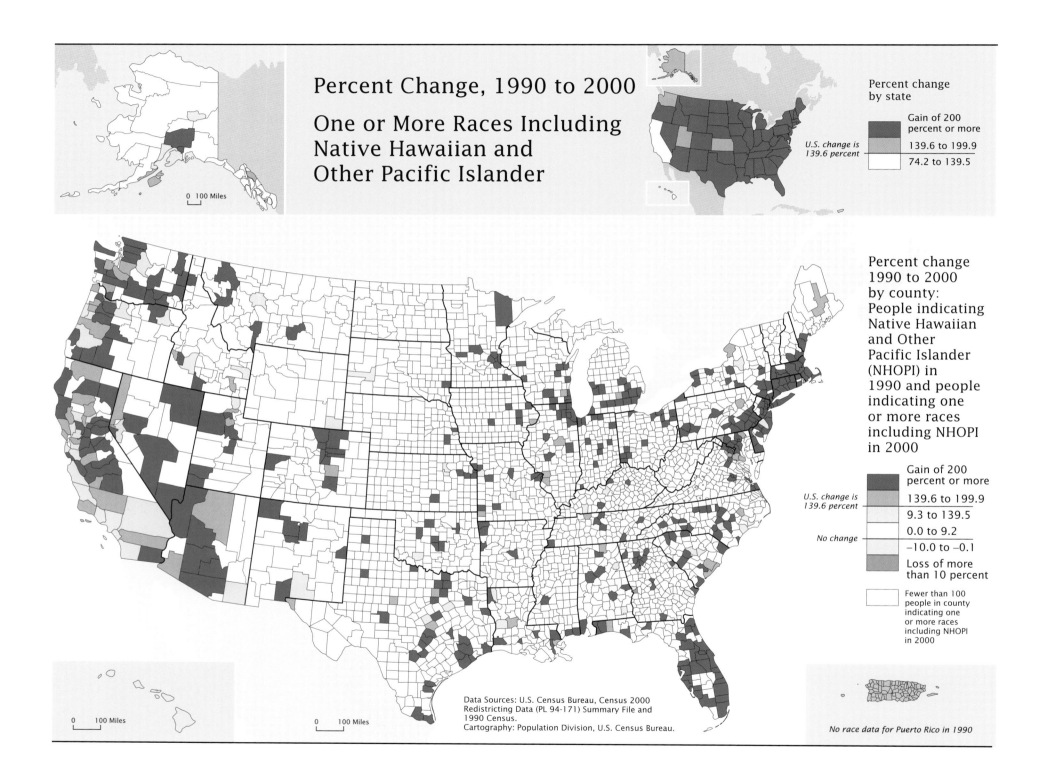

Percent Change, 1990 to 2000

One or More Races Including
Native Hawaiian and
Other Pacific Islander

0   100 Miles

Percent change
by state

U.S. change is
139.6 percent

Gain of 200
percent or more
139.6 to 199.9
74.2 to 139.5

Percent change
1990 to 2000
by county:
People indicating
Native Hawaiian
and Other
Pacific Islander
(NHOPI) in
1990 and people
indicating one
or more races
including NHOPI
in 2000

U.S. change is
139.6 percent

No change

Gain of 200
percent or more
139.6 to 199.9
9.3 to 139.5
0.0 to 9.2
−10.0 to −0.1
Loss of more
than 10 percent

Fewer than 100
people in county
indicating one
or more races
including NHOPI
in 2000

0   100 Miles

0   100 Miles

Data Sources: U.S. Census Bureau, Census 2000
Redistricting Data (PL 94-171) Summary File and
1990 Census.
Cartography: Population Division, U.S. Census Bureau.

No race data for Puerto Rico in 1990

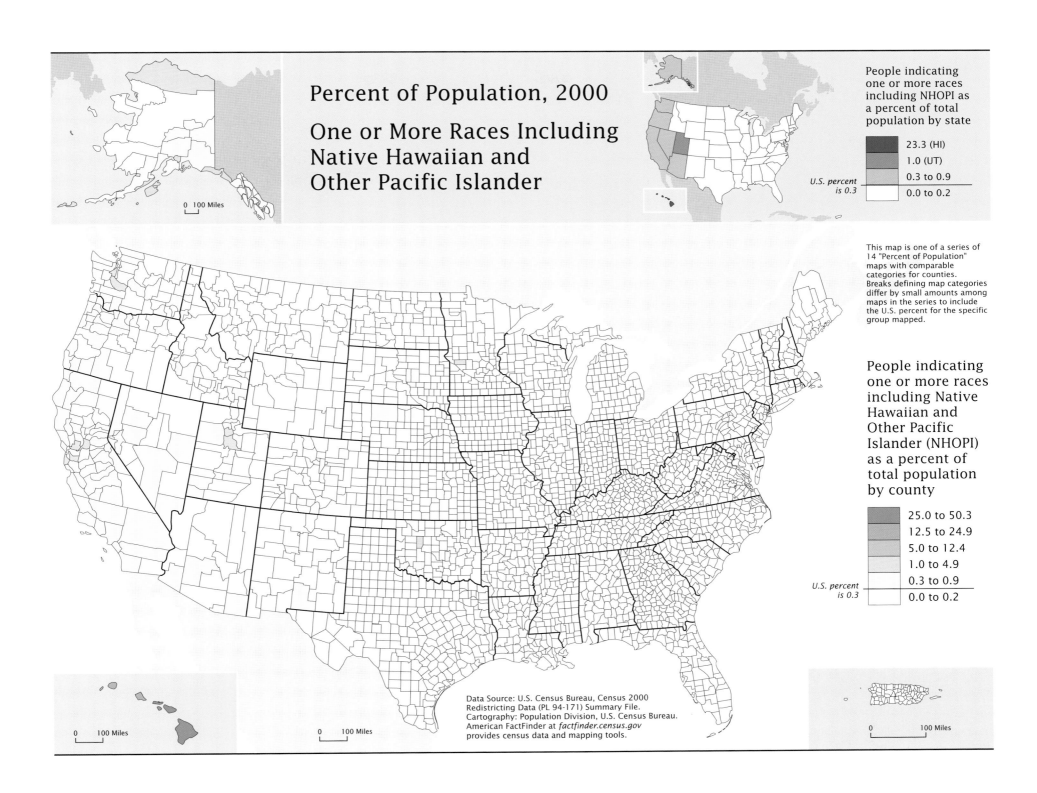

Percent of Population, 2000

One or More Races Including
Native Hawaiian and
Other Pacific Islander

0 100 Miles

People indicating
one or more races
including NHOPI as
a percent of total
population by state

	23.3 (HI)
	1.0 (UT)
	0.3 to 0.9
	0.0 to 0.2

U.S. percent
is 0.3

This map is one of a series of
14 "Percent of Population"
maps with comparable
categories for counties.
Breaks defining map categories
differ by small amounts among
maps in the series to include
the U.S. percent for the specific
group mapped.

People indicating
one or more races
including Native
Hawaiian and
Other Pacific
Islander (NHOPI)
as a percent of
total population
by county

	25.0 to 50.3
	12.5 to 24.9
	5.0 to 12.4
	1.0 to 4.9
	0.3 to 0.9
	0.0 to 0.2

U.S. percent
is 0.3

Data Source: U.S. Census Bureau, Census 2000
Redistricting Data (PL 94-171) Summary File.
Cartography: Population Division, U.S. Census Bureau.
American FactFinder at *factfinder.census.gov*
provides census data and mapping tools.

0 100 Miles

0 100 Miles

0 100 Miles

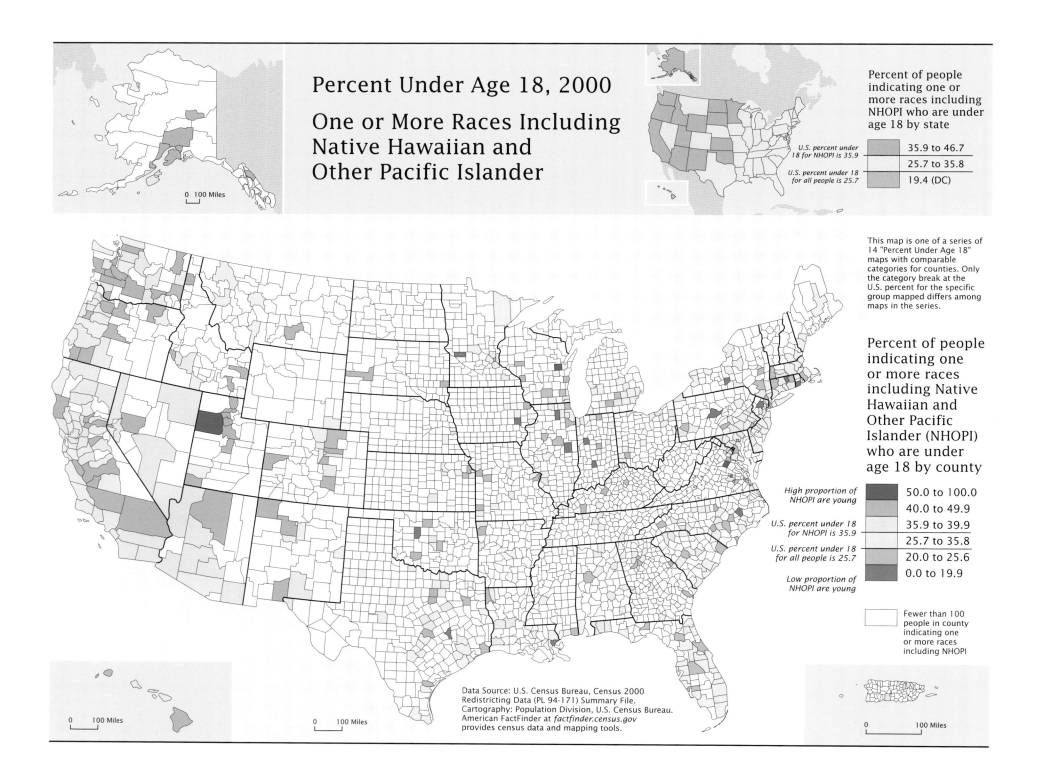

Percent Under Age 18, 2000

One or More Races Including
Native Hawaiian and
Other Pacific Islander

Percent of people
indicating one or
more races including
NHOPI who are under
age 18 by state

*U.S. percent under
18 for NHOPI is 35.9*

*U.S. percent under 18
for all people is 25.7*

	35.9 to 46.7
	25.7 to 35.8
	19.4 (DC)

This map is one of a series of
14 "Percent Under Age 18"
maps with comparable
categories for counties. Only
the category break at the
U.S. percent for the specific
group mapped differs among
maps in the series.

Percent of people
indicating one
or more races
including Native
Hawaiian and
Other Pacific
Islander (NHOPI)
who are under
age 18 by county

*High proportion of
NHOPI are young*

*U.S. percent under 18
for NHOPI is 35.9*

*U.S. percent under 18
for all people is 25.7*

*Low proportion of
NHOPI are young*

	50.0 to 100.0
	40.0 to 49.9
	35.9 to 39.9
	25.7 to 35.8
	20.0 to 25.6
	0.0 to 19.9

Fewer than 100
people in county
indicating one
or more races
including NHOPI

Data Source: U.S. Census Bureau, Census 2000
Redistricting Data (PL 94-171) Summary File.
Cartography: Population Division, U.S. Census Bureau.
American FactFinder at *factfinder.census.gov*
provides census data and mapping tools.

0 100 Miles

0 100 Miles

0 100 Miles

0 100 Miles

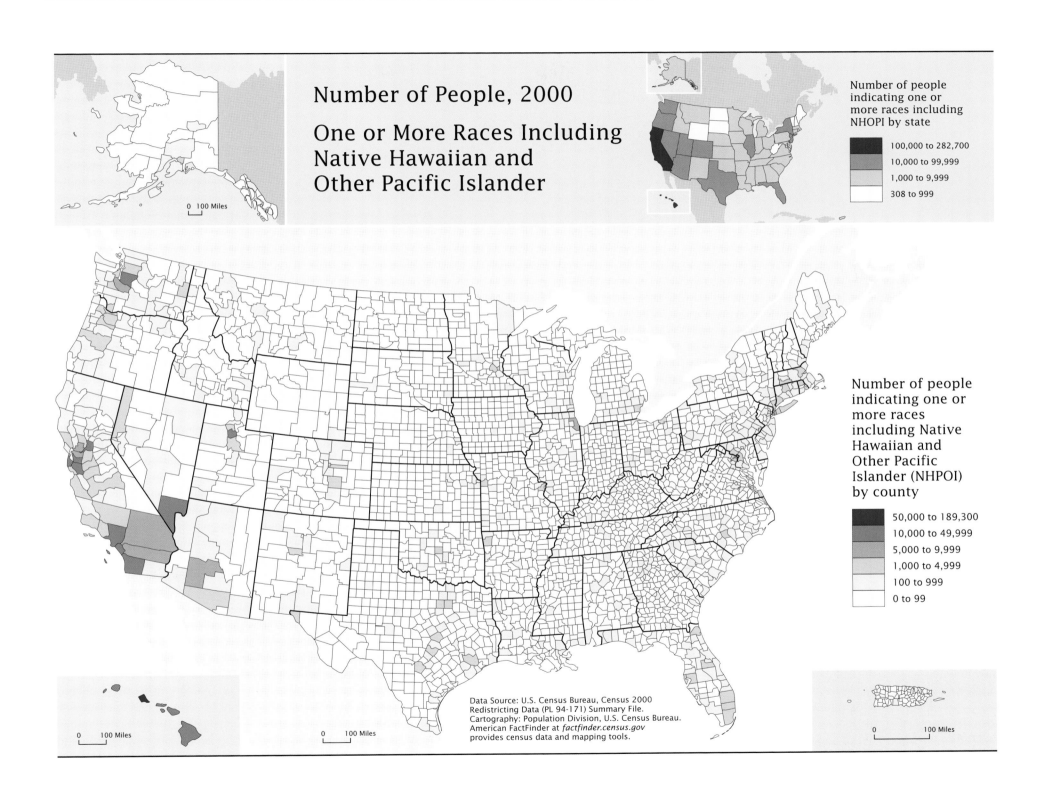

Number of People, 2000

One or More Races Including
Native Hawaiian and
Other Pacific Islander

0 100 Miles

Number of people
indicating one or
more races including
NHOPI by state

■	100,000 to 282,700
▨	10,000 to 99,999
░	1,000 to 9,999
□	308 to 999

Number of people
indicating one or
more races
including Native
Hawaiian and
Other Pacific
Islander (NHPOI)
by county

■	50,000 to 189,300
▨	10,000 to 49,999
▦	5,000 to 9,999
▒	1,000 to 4,999
░	100 to 999
□	0 to 99

0 100 Miles

0 100 Miles

Data Source: U.S. Census Bureau, Census 2000
Redistricting Data (PL 94-171) Summary File.
Cartography: Population Division, U.S. Census Bureau.
American FactFinder at *factfinder.census.gov*
provides census data and mapping tools.

0 100 Miles

Two or More Races

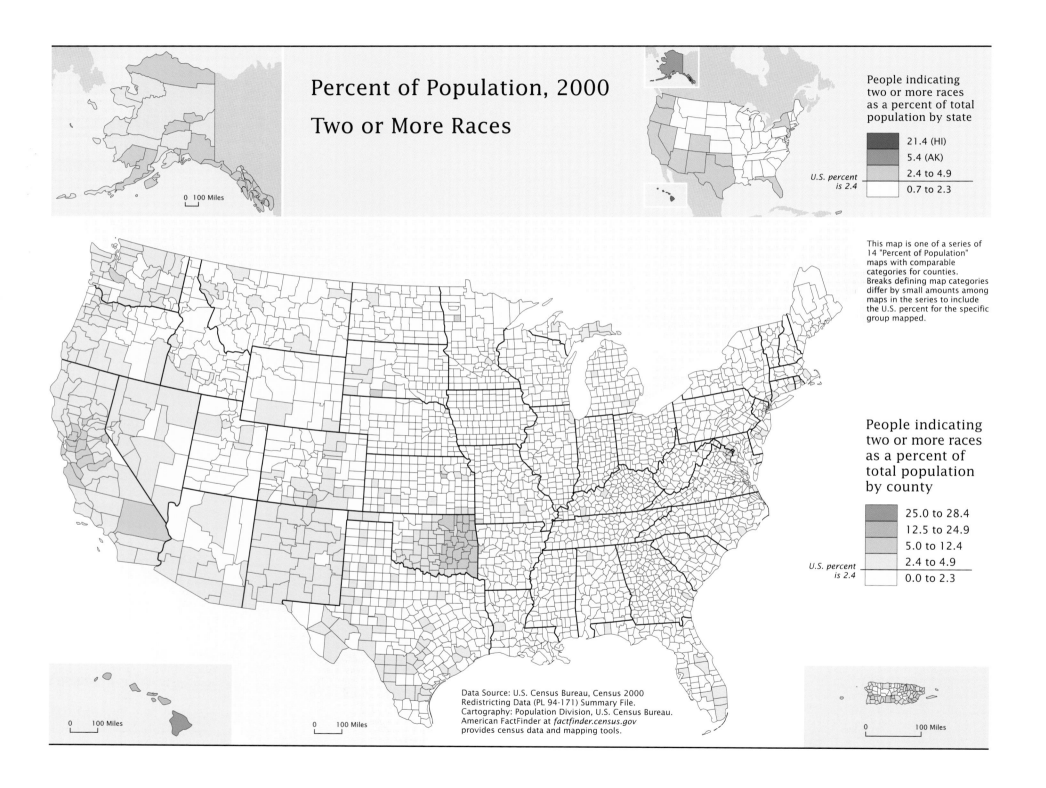

Percent of Population, 2000

Two or More Races

People indicating
two or more races
as a percent of total
population by state

■	21.4 (HI)
■	5.4 (AK)
■	2.4 to 4.9
□	0.7 to 2.3

U.S. percent is 2.4

This map is one of a series of 14 "Percent of Population" maps with comparable categories for counties. Breaks defining map categories differ by small amounts among maps in the series to include the U.S. percent for the specific group mapped.

People indicating
two or more races
as a percent of
total population
by county

■	25.0 to 28.4
■	12.5 to 24.9
■	5.0 to 12.4
■	2.4 to 4.9
□	0.0 to 2.3

U.S. percent is 2.4

0 100 Miles

0 100 Miles

0 100 Miles

Data Source: U.S. Census Bureau, Census 2000 Redistricting Data (PL 94-171) Summary File.
Cartography: Population Division, U.S. Census Bureau.
American FactFinder at *factfinder.census.gov* provides census data and mapping tools.

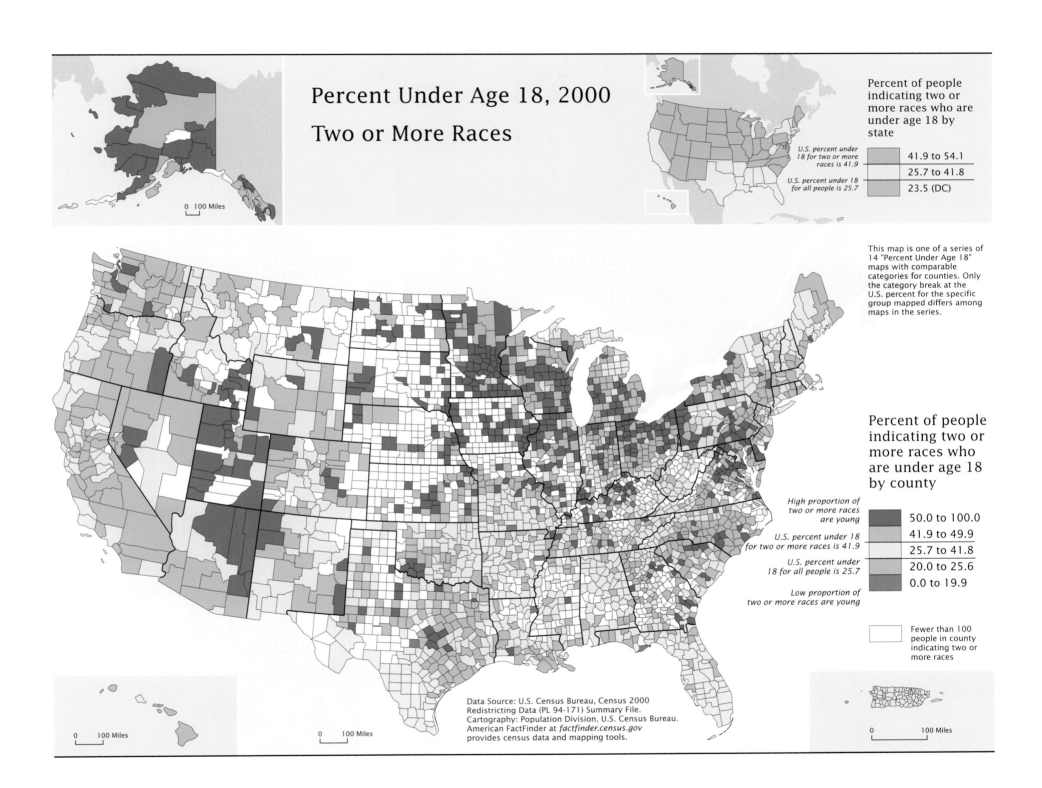

Percent Under Age 18, 2000

Two or More Races

Percent of people indicating two or more races who are under age 18 by state

U.S. percent under 18 for two or more races is 41.9

U.S. percent under 18 for all people is 25.7

41.9 to 54.1
25.7 to 41.8
23.5 (DC)

This map is one of a series of 14 "Percent Under Age 18" maps with comparable categories for counties. Only the category break at the U.S. percent for the specific group mapped differs among maps in the series.

Percent of people indicating two or more races who are under age 18 by county

High proportion of two or more races are young

U.S. percent under 18 for two or more races is 41.9

U.S. percent under 18 for all people is 25.7

Low proportion of two or more races are young

50.0 to 100.0
41.9 to 49.9
25.7 to 41.8
20.0 to 25.6
0.0 to 19.9

Fewer than 100 people in county indicating two or more races

Data Source: U.S. Census Bureau, Census 2000 Redistricting Data (PL 94-171) Summary File. Cartography: Population Division, U.S. Census Bureau. American FactFinder at *factfinder.census.gov* provides census data and mapping tools.

0   100 Miles

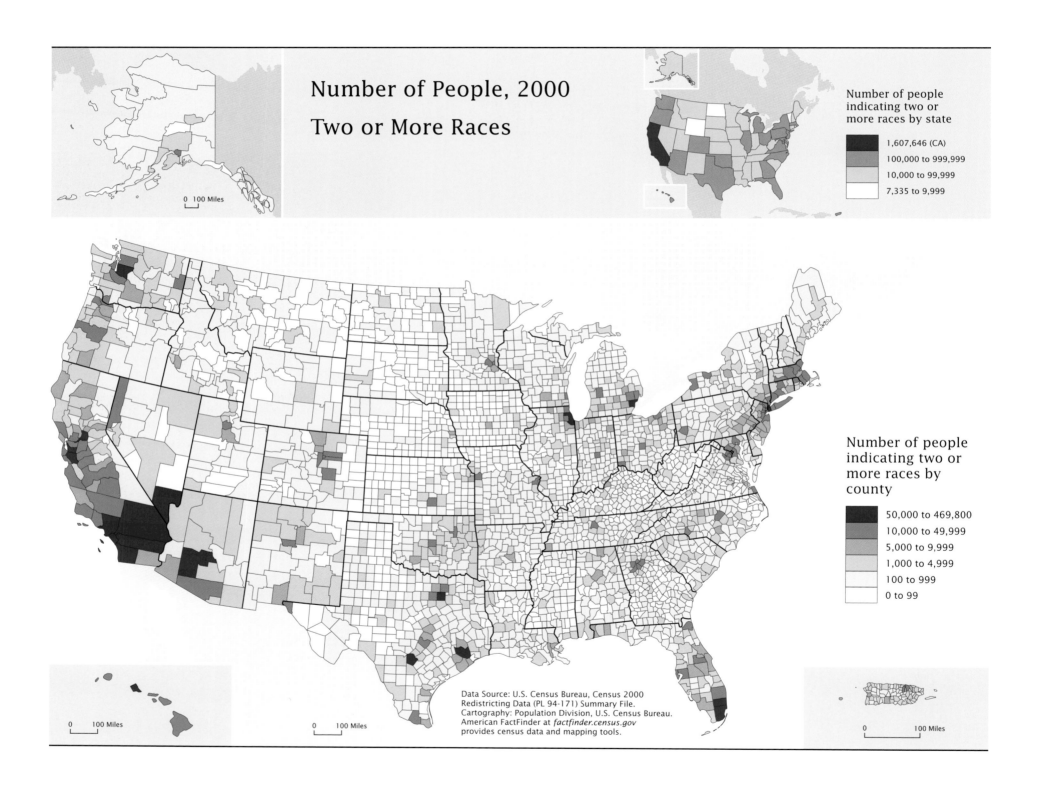

Number of People, 2000

Two or More Races

Number of people indicating two or more races by state

- 1,607,646 (CA)
- 100,000 to 999,999
- 10,000 to 99,999
- 7,335 to 9,999

Number of people indicating two or more races by county

- 50,000 to 469,800
- 10,000 to 49,999
- 5,000 to 9,999
- 1,000 to 4,999
- 100 to 999
- 0 to 99

0 100 Miles

0 100 Miles

0 100 Miles

0 100 Miles

Data Source: U.S. Census Bureau, Census 2000 Redistricting Data (PL 94-171) Summary File. Cartography: Population Division, U.S. Census Bureau. American FactFinder at *factfinder.census.gov* provides census data and mapping tools.

Hispanic or Latino Origin

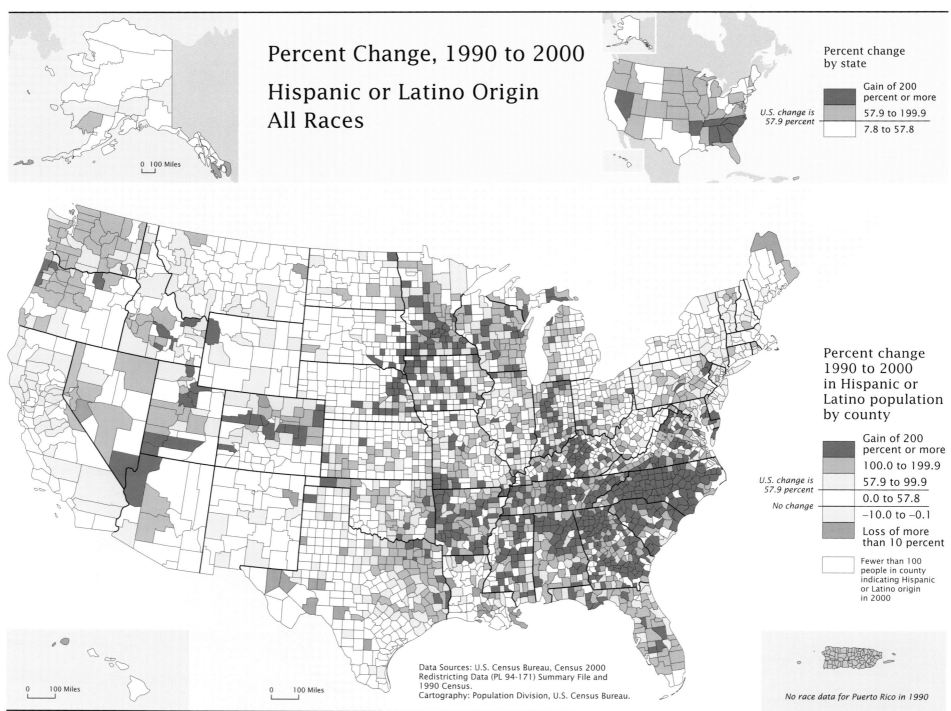

Percent Change, 1990 to 2000

Hispanic or Latino Origin
All Races

Percent change
by state

U.S. change is
57.9 percent

Gain of 200
percent or more
57.9 to 199.9
7.8 to 57.8

Percent change
1990 to 2000
in Hispanic or
Latino population
by county

U.S. change is
57.9 percent

No change

Gain of 200
percent or more
100.0 to 199.9
57.9 to 99.9
0.0 to 57.8
−10.0 to −0.1
Loss of more
than 10 percent

Fewer than 100
people in county
indicating Hispanic
or Latino origin
in 2000

Data Sources: U.S. Census Bureau, Census 2000
Redistricting Data (PL 94-171) Summary File and
1990 Census.
Cartography: Population Division, U.S. Census Bureau.

No race data for Puerto Rico in 1990

0   100 Miles

0   100 Miles

0   100 Miles

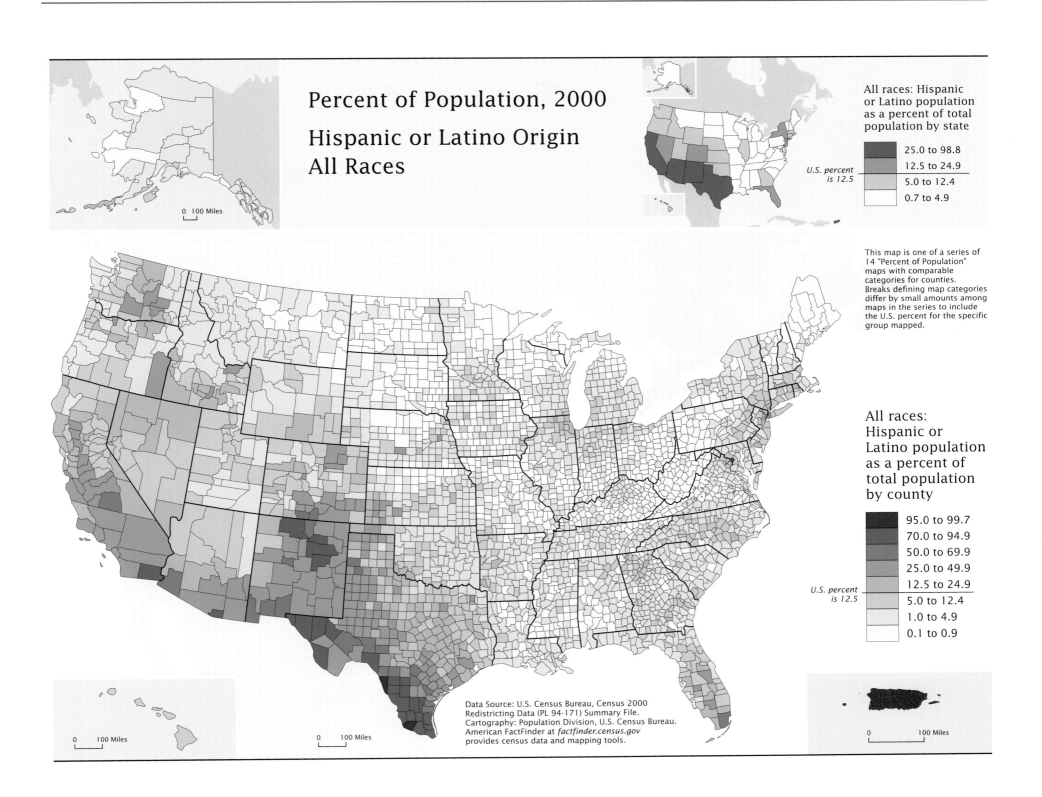

Percent of Population, 2000

Hispanic or Latino Origin
All Races

0   100 Miles

All races: Hispanic or Latino population as a percent of total population by state

	25.0 to 98.8
	12.5 to 24.9
	5.0 to 12.4
	0.7 to 4.9

U.S. percent is 12.5

This map is one of a series of 14 "Percent of Population" maps with comparable categories for counties. Breaks defining map categories differ by small amounts among maps in the series to include the U.S. percent for the specific group mapped.

All races: Hispanic or Latino population as a percent of total population by county

	95.0 to 99.7
	70.0 to 94.9
	50.0 to 69.9
	25.0 to 49.9
	12.5 to 24.9
	5.0 to 12.4
	1.0 to 4.9
	0.1 to 0.9

U.S. percent is 12.5

Data Source: U.S. Census Bureau, Census 2000 Redistricting Data (PL 94-171) Summary File.
Cartography: Population Division, U.S. Census Bureau. American FactFinder at *factfinder.census.gov* provides census data and mapping tools.

0   100 Miles

0   100 Miles

0   100 Miles

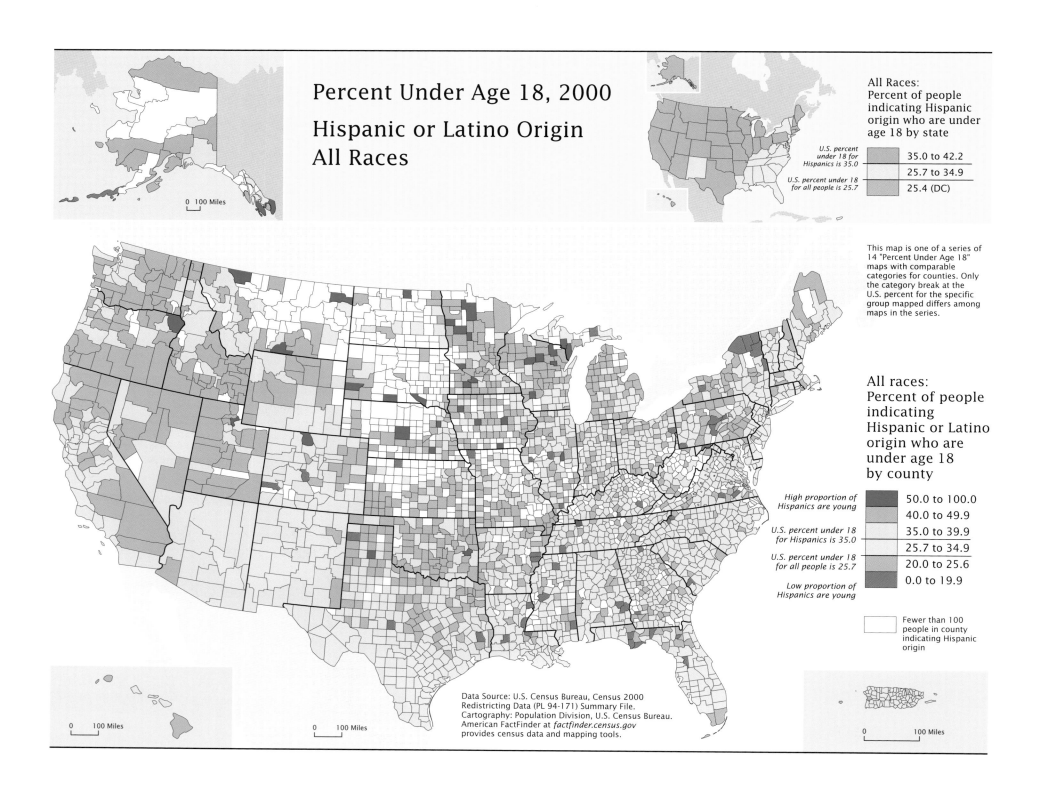

Percent Under Age 18, 2000

Hispanic or Latino Origin
All Races

All Races:
Percent of people indicating Hispanic origin who are under age 18 by state

U.S. percent under 18 for Hispanics is 35.0 — 35.0 to 42.2

25.7 to 34.9

U.S. percent under 18 for all people is 25.7 — 25.4 (DC)

This map is one of a series of 14 "Percent Under Age 18" maps with comparable categories for counties. Only the category break at the U.S. percent for the specific group mapped differs among maps in the series.

All races:
Percent of people indicating Hispanic or Latino origin who are under age 18 by county

High proportion of Hispanics are young — 50.0 to 100.0

40.0 to 49.9

U.S. percent under 18 for Hispanics is 35.0 — 35.0 to 39.9

25.7 to 34.9

U.S. percent under 18 for all people is 25.7 — 20.0 to 25.6

Low proportion of Hispanics are young — 0.0 to 19.9

Fewer than 100 people in county indicating Hispanic origin

0 100 Miles

Data Source: U.S. Census Bureau, Census 2000 Redistricting Data (PL 94-171) Summary File.
Cartography: Population Division, U.S. Census Bureau.
American FactFinder at *factfinder.census.gov* provides census data and mapping tools.

0 100 Miles

0 100 Miles

0 100 Miles

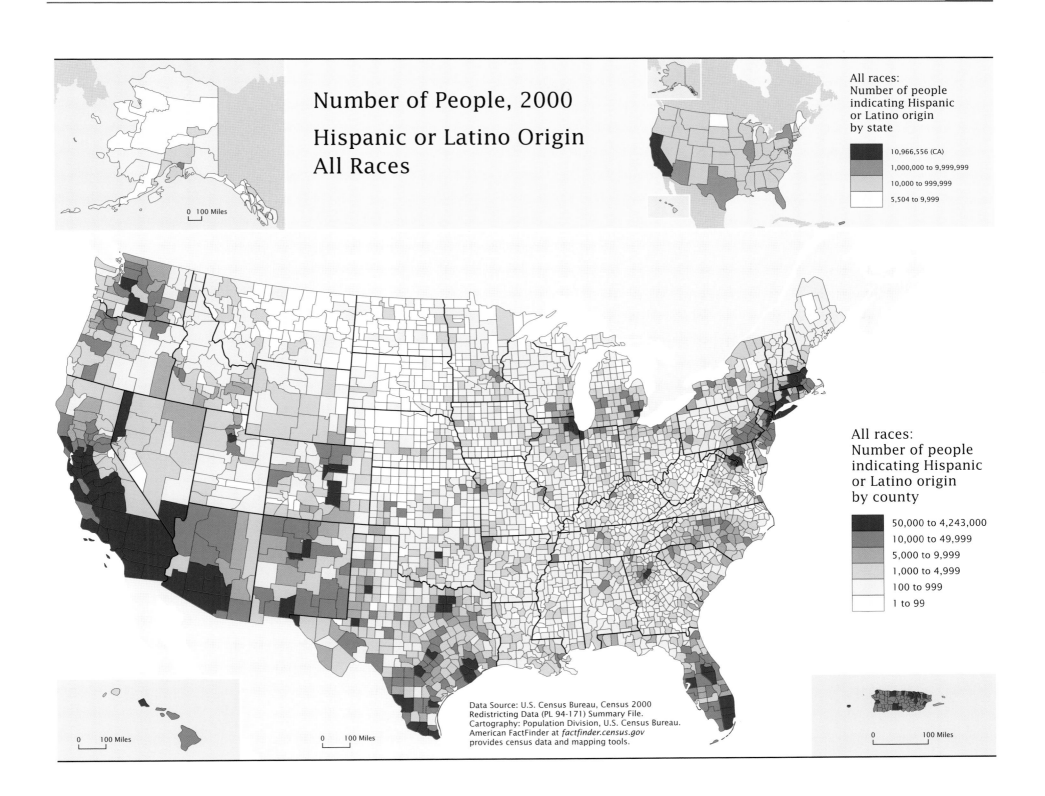

Number of People, 2000

Hispanic or Latino Origin
All Races

All races:
Number of people
indicating Hispanic
or Latino origin
by state

10,966,556 (CA)
1,000,000 to 9,999,999
10,000 to 999,999
5,504 to 9,999

All races:
Number of people
indicating Hispanic
or Latino origin
by county

50,000 to 4,243,000
10,000 to 49,999
5,000 to 9,999
1,000 to 4,999
100 to 999
1 to 99

0 100 Miles

0 100 Miles

0 100 Miles

0 100 Miles

Data Source: U.S. Census Bureau, Census 2000
Redistricting Data (PL 94-171) Summary File.
Cartography: Population Division, U.S. Census Bureau.
American FactFinder at *factfinder.census.gov*
provides census data and mapping tools.

White, Not Hispanic or Latino Origin

One race: **White, Not Hispanic or Latino Origin**

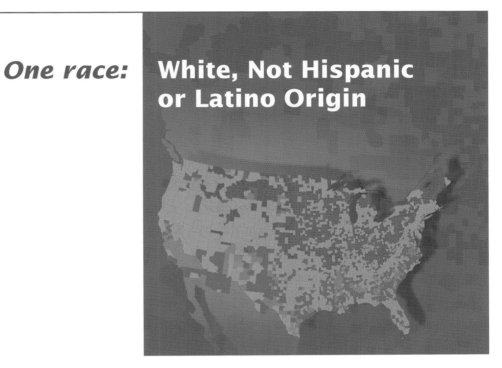

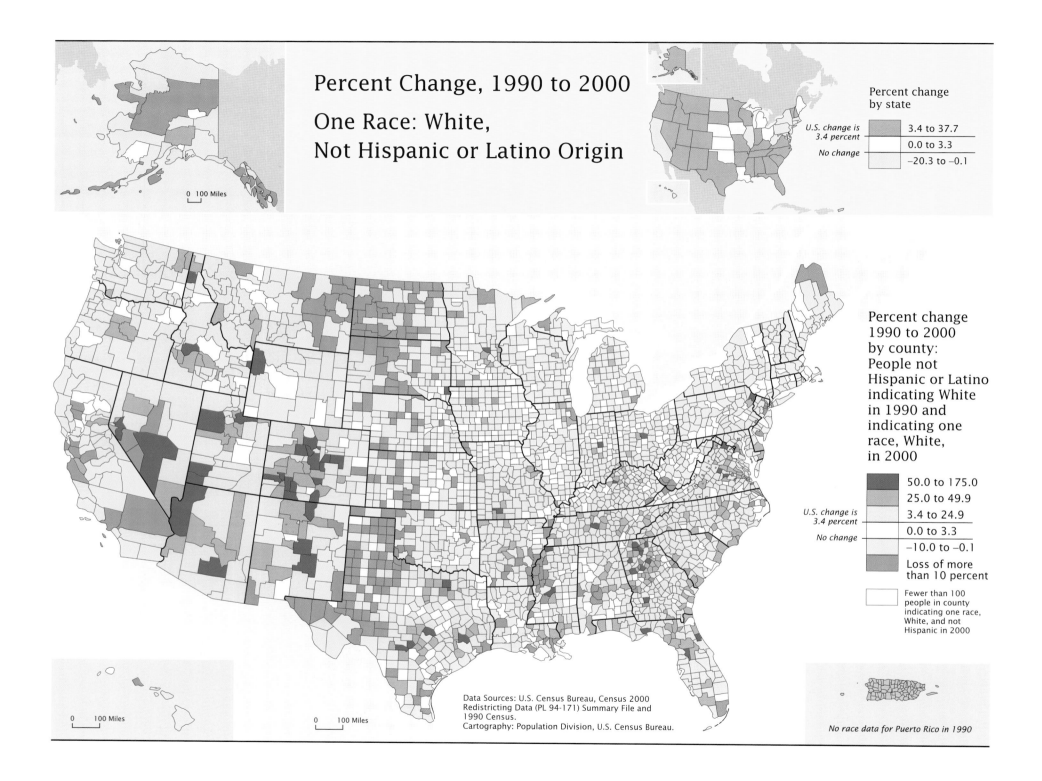

Percent Change, 1990 to 2000

One Race: White,
Not Hispanic or Latino Origin

Percent change
by state

U.S. change is
3.4 percent

No change

3.4 to 37.7

0.0 to 3.3

−20.3 to −0.1

Percent change
1990 to 2000
by county:
People not
Hispanic or Latino
indicating White
in 1990 and
indicating one
race, White,
in 2000

50.0 to 175.0

25.0 to 49.9

U.S. change is
3.4 percent

3.4 to 24.9

0.0 to 3.3

No change

−10.0 to −0.1

Loss of more
than 10 percent

Fewer than 100
people in county
indicating one race,
White, and not
Hispanic in 2000

0   100 Miles

0   100 Miles

0   100 Miles

Data Sources: U.S. Census Bureau, Census 2000
Redistricting Data (PL 94-171) Summary File and
1990 Census.
Cartography: Population Division, U.S. Census Bureau.

No race data for Puerto Rico in 1990

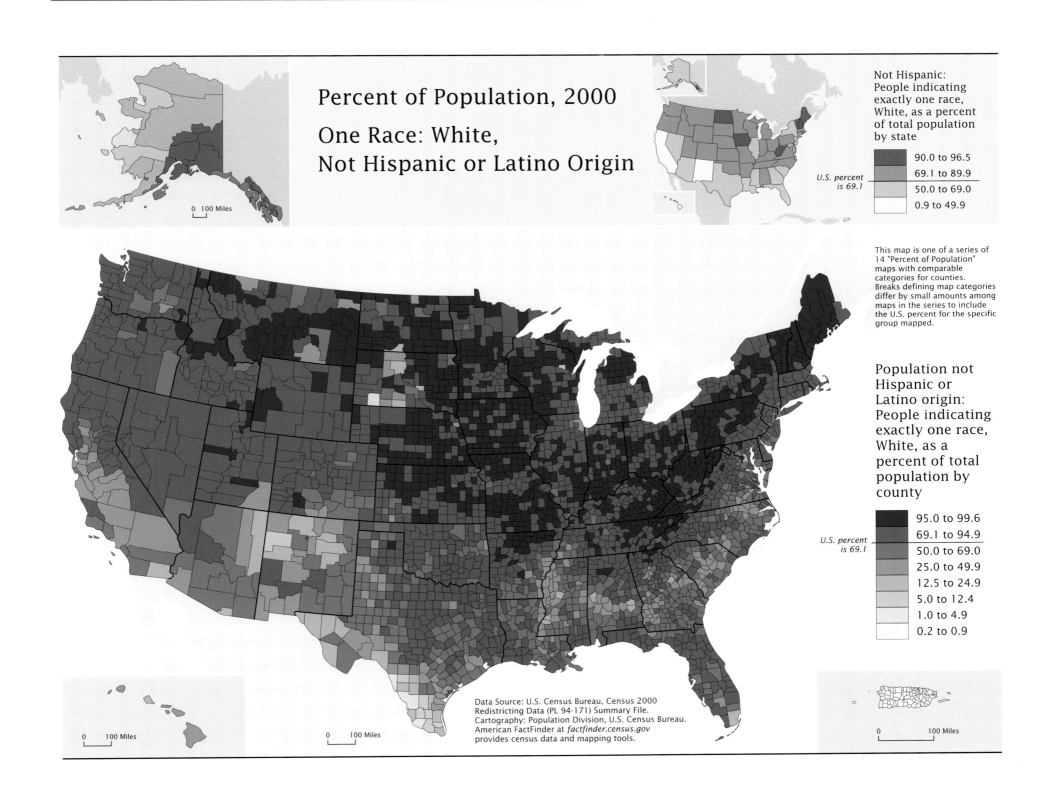

Percent of Population, 2000

One Race: White,
Not Hispanic or Latino Origin

Not Hispanic:
People indicating
exactly one race,
White, as a percent
of total population
by state

U.S. percent
is 69.1

	90.0 to 96.5
	69.1 to 89.9
	50.0 to 69.0
	0.9 to 49.9

This map is one of a series of
14 "Percent of Population"
maps with comparable
categories for counties.
Breaks defining map categories
differ by small amounts among
maps in the series to include
the U.S. percent for the specific
group mapped.

Population not
Hispanic or
Latino origin:
People indicating
exactly one race,
White, as a
percent of total
population by
county

U.S. percent
is 69.1

	95.0 to 99.6
	69.1 to 94.9
	50.0 to 69.0
	25.0 to 49.9
	12.5 to 24.9
	5.0 to 12.4
	1.0 to 4.9
	0.2 to 0.9

0   100 Miles

Data Source: U.S. Census Bureau, Census 2000
Redistricting Data (PL 94-171) Summary File.
Cartography: Population Division, U.S. Census Bureau.
American FactFinder at *factfinder.census.gov*
provides census data and mapping tools.

0   100 Miles

0   100 Miles

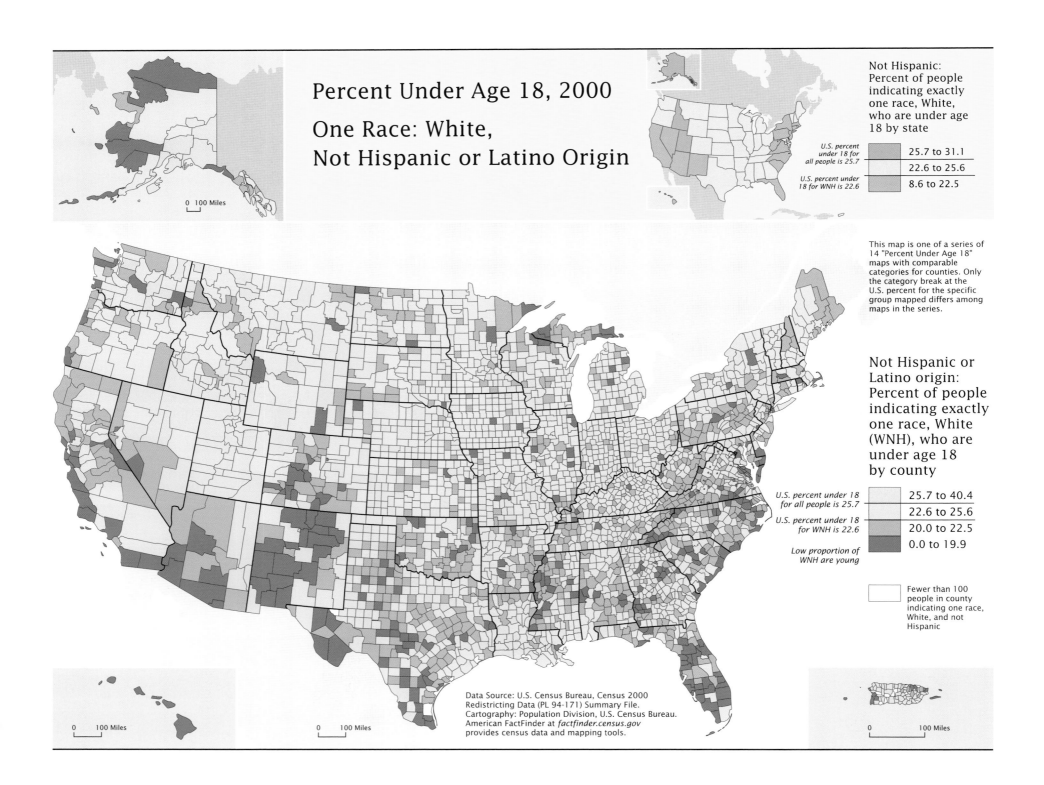

Percent Under Age 18, 2000

One Race: White,
Not Hispanic or Latino Origin

Not Hispanic:
Percent of people
indicating exactly
one race, White,
who are under age
18 by state

U.S. percent
under 18 for
all people is 25.7

U.S. percent under
18 for WNH is 22.6

| 25.7 to 31.1 |
| 22.6 to 25.6 |
| 8.6 to 22.5 |

This map is one of a series of 14 "Percent Under Age 18" maps with comparable categories for counties. Only the category break at the U.S. percent for the specific group mapped differs among maps in the series.

Not Hispanic or
Latino origin:
Percent of people
indicating exactly
one race, White
(WNH), who are
under age 18
by county

U.S. percent under 18
for all people is 25.7

U.S. percent under 18
for WNH is 22.6

Low proportion of
WNH are young

| 25.7 to 40.4 |
| 22.6 to 25.6 |
| 20.0 to 22.5 |
| 0.0 to 19.9 |

Fewer than 100
people in county
indicating one race,
White, and not
Hispanic

Data Source: U.S. Census Bureau, Census 2000 Redistricting Data (PL 94-171) Summary File. Cartography: Population Division, U.S. Census Bureau. American FactFinder at *factfinder.census.gov* provides census data and mapping tools.

0 100 Miles

0 100 Miles

0 100 Miles

0 100 Miles

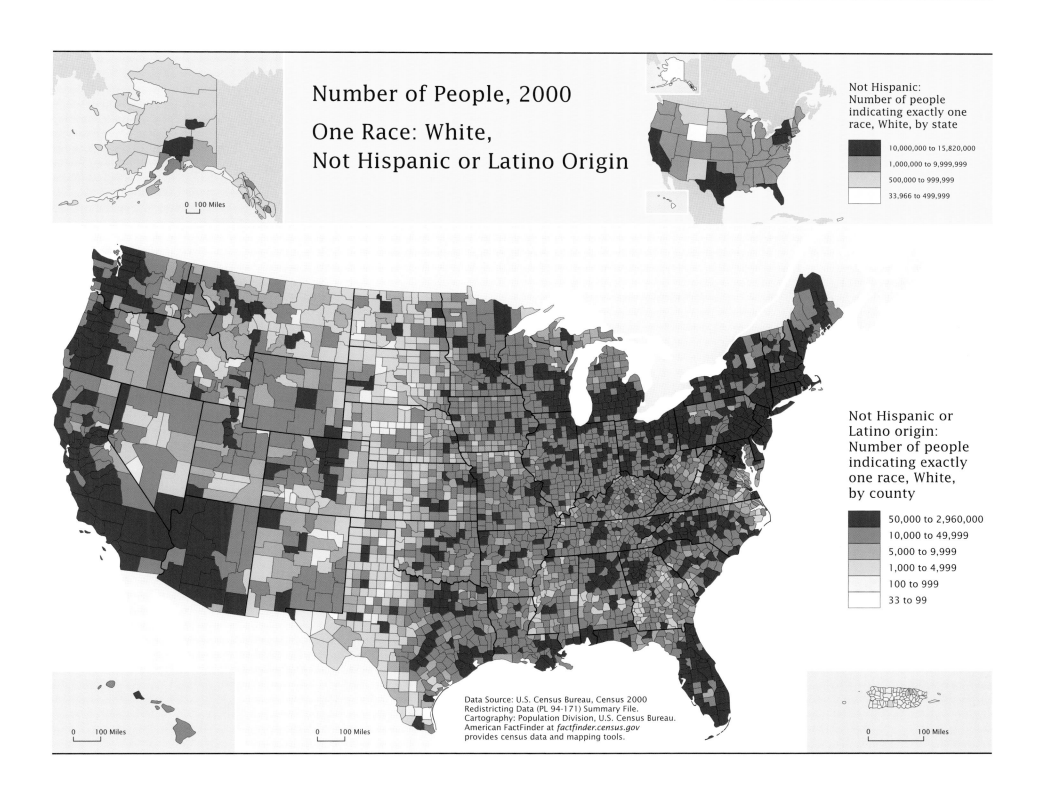

Number of People, 2000

One Race: White,
Not Hispanic or Latino Origin

Not Hispanic:
Number of people
indicating exactly one
race, White, by state

- 10,000,000 to 15,820,000
- 1,000,000 to 9,999,999
- 500,000 to 999,999
- 33,966 to 499,999

Not Hispanic or
Latino origin:
Number of people
indicating exactly
one race, White,
by county

- 50,000 to 2,960,000
- 10,000 to 49,999
- 5,000 to 9,999
- 1,000 to 4,999
- 100 to 999
- 33 to 99

Data Source: U.S. Census Bureau, Census 2000
Redistricting Data (PL 94-171) Summary File.
Cartography: Population Division, U.S. Census Bureau.
American FactFinder at *factfinder.census.gov*
provides census data and mapping tools.

0 100 Miles

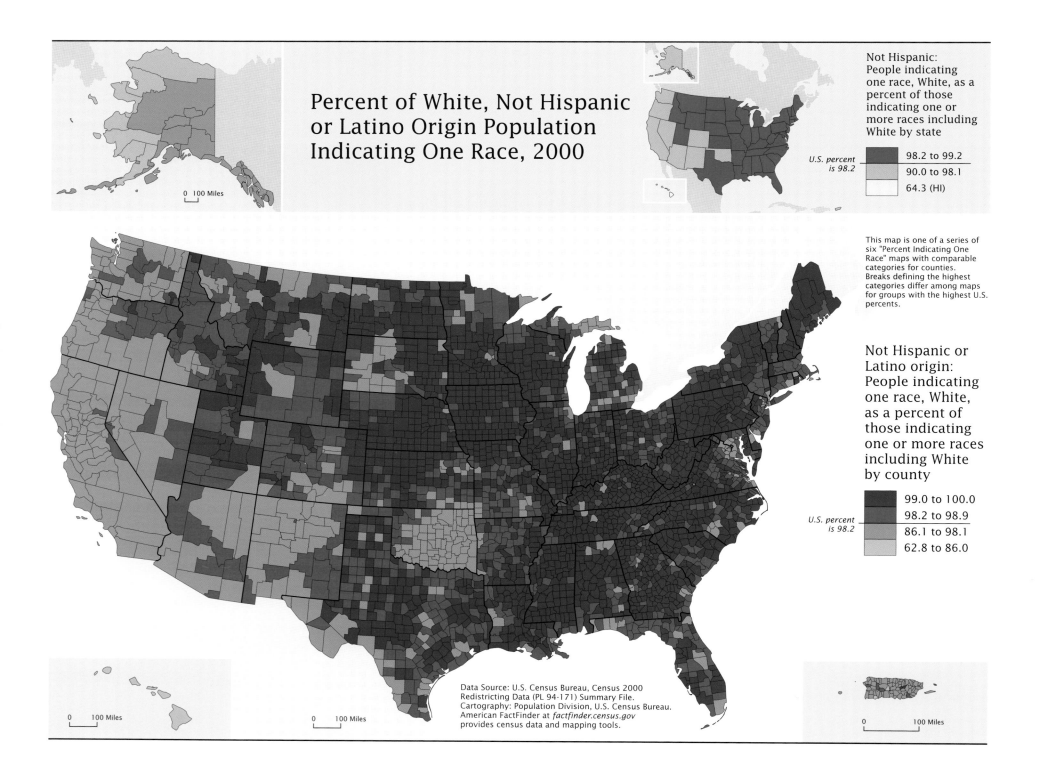

Percent of White, Not Hispanic or Latino Origin Population Indicating One Race, 2000

Not Hispanic: People indicating one race, White, as a percent of those indicating one or more races including White by state

U.S. percent is 98.2

	98.2 to 99.2
	90.0 to 98.1
	64.3 (HI)

This map is one of a series of six "Percent Indicating One Race" maps with comparable categories for counties. Breaks defining the highest categories differ among maps for groups with the highest U.S. percents.

Not Hispanic or Latino origin: People indicating one race, White, as a percent of those indicating one or more races including White by county

	99.0 to 100.0
	98.2 to 98.9
U.S. percent is 98.2	86.1 to 98.1
	62.8 to 86.0

Data Source: U.S. Census Bureau, Census 2000 Redistricting Data (PL 94-171) Summary File. Cartography: Population Division, U.S. Census Bureau. American FactFinder at *factfinder.census.gov* provides census data and mapping tools.

0 100 Miles

White, Not Hispanic or Latino Origin

One or more races including

White, Not Hispanic or Latino Origin

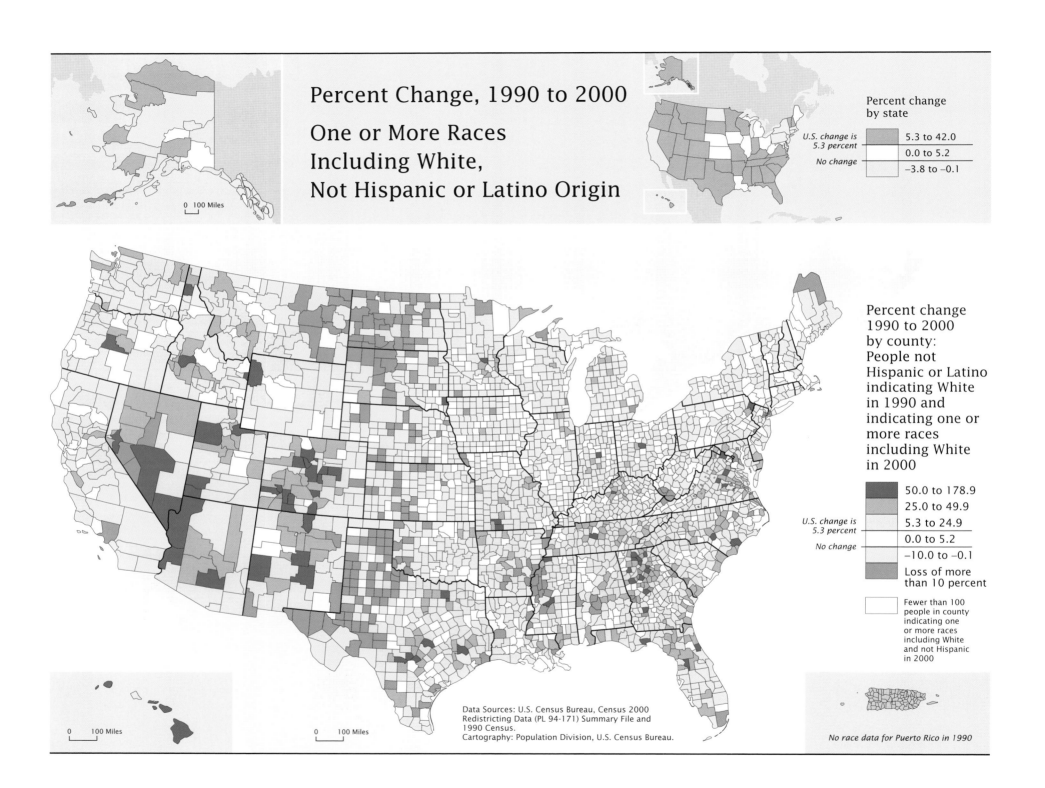

Percent Change, 1990 to 2000

One or More Races
Including White,
Not Hispanic or Latino Origin

Percent change
by state

U.S. change is
5.3 percent

No change

5.3 to 42.0
0.0 to 5.2
−3.8 to −0.1

0 100 Miles

Percent change
1990 to 2000
by county:
People not
Hispanic or Latino
indicating White
in 1990 and
indicating one or
more races
including White
in 2000

U.S. change is
5.3 percent

No change

50.0 to 178.9
25.0 to 49.9
5.3 to 24.9
0.0 to 5.2
−10.0 to −0.1
Loss of more
than 10 percent

Fewer than 100
people in county
indicating one
or more races
including White
and not Hispanic
in 2000

0 100 Miles

0 100 Miles

Data Sources: U.S. Census Bureau, Census 2000
Redistricting Data (PL 94-171) Summary File and
1990 Census.
Cartography: Population Division, U.S. Census Bureau.

No race data for Puerto Rico in 1990

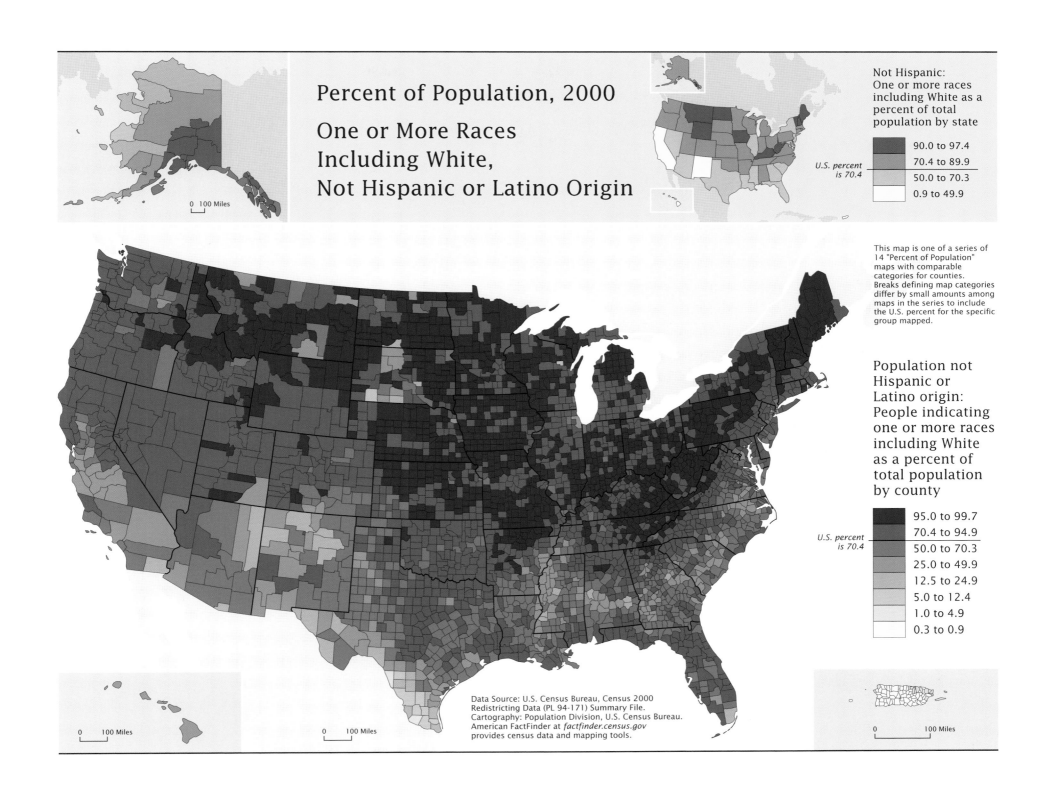

Percent of Population, 2000

One or More Races Including White, Not Hispanic or Latino Origin

Not Hispanic: One or more races including White as a percent of total population by state

U.S. percent is 70.4

	90.0 to 97.4
	70.4 to 89.9
	50.0 to 70.3
	0.9 to 49.9

This map is one of a series of 14 "Percent of Population" maps with comparable categories for counties. Breaks defining map categories differ by small amounts among maps in the series to include the U.S. percent for the specific group mapped.

Population not Hispanic or Latino origin: People indicating one or more races including White as a percent of total population by county

U.S. percent is 70.4

	95.0 to 99.7
	70.4 to 94.9
	50.0 to 70.3
	25.0 to 49.9
	12.5 to 24.9
	5.0 to 12.4
	1.0 to 4.9
	0.3 to 0.9

0 100 Miles

0 100 Miles

0 100 Miles

0 100 Miles

Data Source: U.S. Census Bureau, Census 2000 Redistricting Data (PL 94-171) Summary File. Cartography: Population Division, U.S. Census Bureau. American FactFinder at *factfinder.census.gov* provides census data and mapping tools.

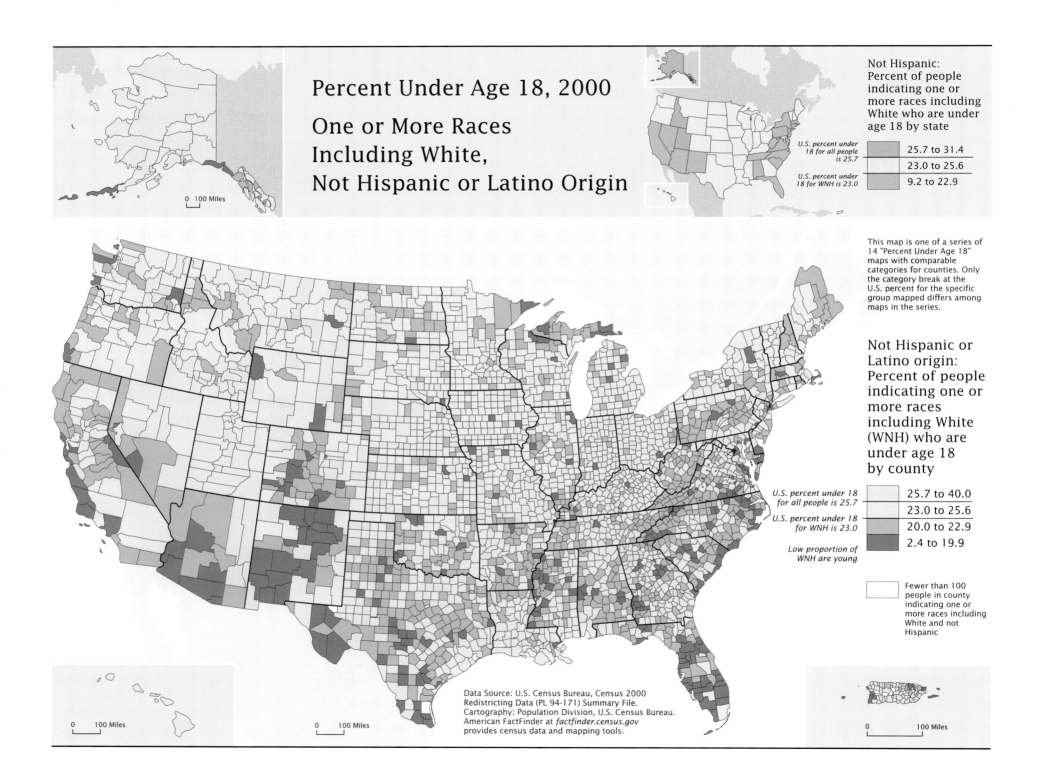

Percent Under Age 18, 2000

One or More Races
Including White,
Not Hispanic or Latino Origin

Not Hispanic:
Percent of people
indicating one or
more races including
White who are under
age 18 by state

U.S. percent under
18 for all people
is 25.7

U.S. percent under
18 for WNH is 23.0

	25.7 to 31.4
	23.0 to 25.6
	9.2 to 22.9

This map is one of a series of
14 "Percent Under Age 18"
maps with comparable
categories for counties. Only
the category break at the
U.S. percent for the specific
group mapped differs among
maps in the series.

Not Hispanic or
Latino origin:
Percent of people
indicating one or
more races
including White
(WNH) who are
under age 18
by county

U.S. percent under 18
for all people is 25.7

U.S. percent under 18
for WNH is 23.0

Low proportion of
WNH are young

	25.7 to 40.0
	23.0 to 25.6
	20.0 to 22.9
	2.4 to 19.9

Fewer than 100
people in county
indicating one or
more races including
White and not
Hispanic

Data Source: U.S. Census Bureau, Census 2000
Redistricting Data (PL 94-171) Summary File.
Cartography: Population Division, U.S. Census Bureau.
American FactFinder at *factfinder.census.gov*
provides census data and mapping tools.

0 100 Miles

0 100 Miles

0 100 Miles

0 100 Miles

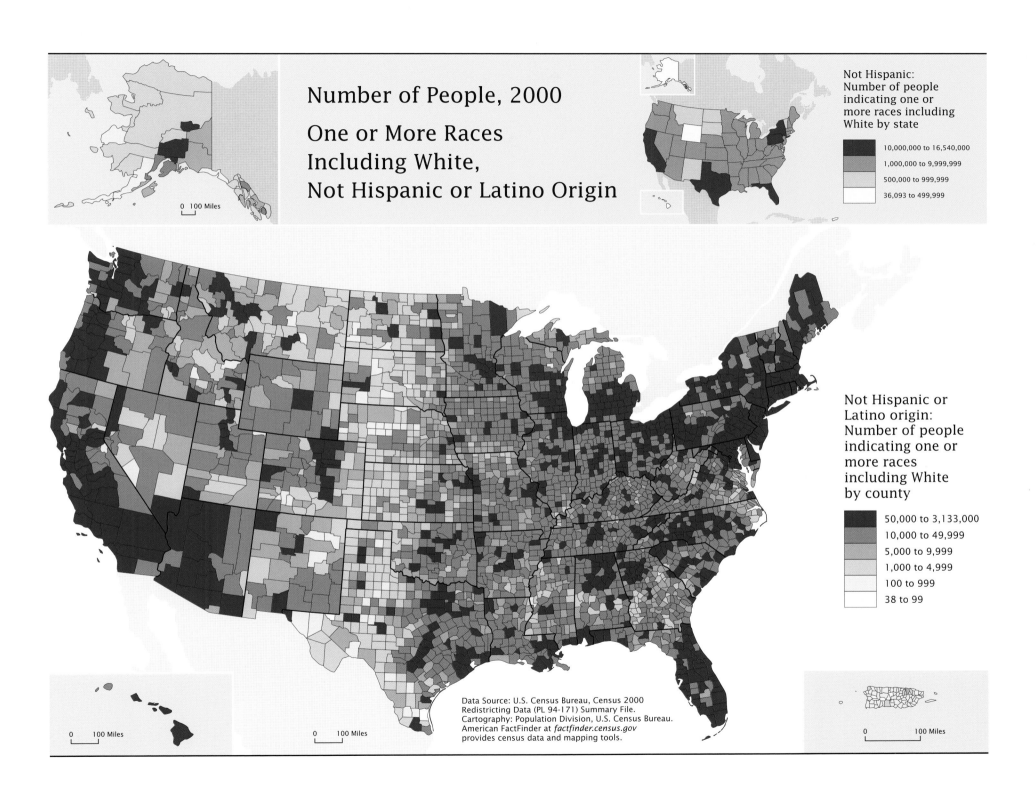

Number of People, 2000

One or More Races
Including White,
Not Hispanic or Latino Origin

Not Hispanic:
Number of people
indicating one or
more races including
White by state

10,000,000 to 16,540,000
1,000,000 to 9,999,999
500,000 to 999,999
36,093 to 499,999

Not Hispanic or
Latino origin:
Number of people
indicating one or
more races
including White
by county

50,000 to 3,133,000
10,000 to 49,999
5,000 to 9,999
1,000 to 4,999
100 to 999
38 to 99

0 100 Miles

0 100 Miles

0 100 Miles

0 100 Miles

Data Source: U.S. Census Bureau, Census 2000
Redistricting Data (PL 94-171) Summary File.
Cartography: Population Division, U.S. Census Bureau.
American FactFinder at *factfinder.census.gov*
provides census data and mapping tools.

Bibliography

The authors examined a wide range of country, state, and specialized atlases that included population themes. For readers interested in other, innovative approaches to the topic or to good standard data presentation, we recommend the following titles.

Allen, James Paul, and Eugene James Turner, 1988, *We the People: An Atlas of America's Ethnic Diversity*, Macmillan, New York.

Champion, Tony, Cecilia Wong, Ann Rooke, Daniel Dorling, Mike Coombes, and Chris Brunsdon, 1996, *The Population of Britain in the 1990s: A Social and Economic Atlas*, Clarendon Press, Oxford.

Chiriin, Kokudo, 1990, *The National Atlas of Japan*, Japan Map Center, Tokyo.

Dean, William G., and Geoffrey J. Matthews, 1969, *Economic Atlas of Ontario*, University of Toronto Press, Toronto.

Department of Energy, Mines and Resources, Canada, 1974, *The National Atlas of Canada* (4th edition), Macmillan of Canada, Toronto.

Donley, Michael W., Stuart Allan, Patricia Caro, and Clyde P. Patton, 1979, *Atlas of California*, Pacific Book Center, Culver City, California.

Dorling, Daniel, 1995, *A New Social Atlas of Britain*, John Wiley & Sons, Chichester, England.

Doyle, Rodger, 1994, *Atlas of Contemporary America: Portraits of a Nation*, Facts on File, New York.

Fernald, Edward A., and Elizabeth D. Purdum (editors), 1996, *Atlas of Florida* (revised edition), University Press of Florida, Gainesville.

Gannett, Henry, 1903, *Statistical Atlas*, United States Census Office, Washington, D.C.

Gan Ziyu (editor), 1994, *The National Economic Atlas of China*, Oxford University Press, Oxford.

Mattson, Mark T., 1992, *Atlas of the 1990 Census*, Macmillan, New York.

Gerlach, Arch C. (editor), 1970, *The National Atlas of the United States of America*, U.S. Geological Survey, Washington, D.C.

Öberg, Sture, and Peter Springfeldt, 1991, *National Atlas of Sweden: The Population*, SNA Publishing, Stockholm.

Pickle, Linda Williams, Michael Mungiole, Gretchen K. Jones, and Andrew A. White, 1996, *Atlas of United States Mortality*, National Center for Health Statistics, Hyattsville, Maryland.

Prucha, Francis Paul, 1990, *Atlas of American Indian Affairs*, University of Nebraska Press, Lincoln.

Riebsame, William E. (editor), 1997, *Atlas of the New West: Portrait of a Changing Region*, W. W. Norton, New York.

Tait, Nick, Andrew Whiteford, Jané Joubert, Johan van Zyl, Dulcie Krige, and Basil Pillay, 1996, *A Socio-Economic Atlas of South Africa: A Demographic, Socio-Economic and Cultural Profile of South Africa*, HSRC Publishers (Human Sciences Research Council), Pretoria.

Turner, Eugene, and James P. Allen, 1990, *An Atlas of Population Patterns in Metropolitan Los Angeles*, Occasional Publications in Geography No. 8, Department of Geography, California State University, Northridge, California.

Mapping Census 2000: The Geography of U.S. Diversity
Book and cover design and production   Jennifer Galloway
Copyediting   Michael Hyatt
Printing coordination   Cliff Crabbe

The maps in this atlas were created by the U.S. Census Bureau using ESRI ArcMap 8.1
Prerelease software. The maps were exported from ArcMap as Adobe® Illustrator® files
using a beta version of ArcMap software's Adobe Illustrator export driver. The text
was set in Lucida Serif and Lucida Sans.